D1630017

SECRETS OF
French Sauces

OVER 100 AUTHENTIC SAUCE RECIPES

General Editor · Beverly LeBlanc

Macdonald Orbis

A Macdonald Orbis BOOK

Based upon the *Grand Livre de la Cuisine,* © Edition No 1, Paris 1982
English text and design © Macdonald & Co (Publishers) Ltd 1986, 1988
First published in Great Britain in 1988
by Macdonald & Co (Publishers) Ltd
London & Sydney

A member of Pergamon MCC Publishing Corporation plc

British Library Cataloguing in Publication Data
    LeBlanc, Beverly
    Secrets of French Sauces
    1. Sauces
    I. Title
    641.8'14   TX819.A1

ISBN 0-356-15318-5

Illustrated by Claire Harper

Designer: Clair Lidzey

Macdonald & Co (Publishers) Ltd
Greater London House
Hampstead Road
London NW1 7QX

Printed and bound in Great Britain by
Purnell Book Production Ltd, Paulton, Bristol
A member of BPCC plc

CONTENTS

Symbols

The symbols show how easy a recipe is, and the preparation and cooking times:-

easy

more difficult

for experienced cooks

preparation time

cooking time

When using this book, remember the following points: (1) all quantities are for four people unless otherwise stated (2) use only one set of ingredients for the recipes, since American, imperial and metric ingredients are not exact equivalents and (3) in the text of the recipes, American quantities and ingredients are listed first, with the British equivalents in square brackets.

INTRODUCTION

Given any food, no matter if it is of the highest quality and cooked to perfection, without a sauce it is incomplete, an unfinished masterpiece, half the dish it could be. A glorious mixture of subtle flavours, sauces are said to be the chef's secret, the key to his individuality and a chance for him to impart a personal impression of what is often a standard recipe. Once the basic principles are understood, sauces can evolve from other sauces and become the saucier's personal property. In this book, there are recipes for all the basic sauces and many variations on any particular theme. From the simplest butter sauces to the multi-faceted flavours of a grand stock-based sauce, they are all collected here. Learn how to make mayonnaise and marvel at how much oil those egg yolks can absorb; take in the heady aroma of crushed basil when making pesto. Get to grips with stocks and remember these are the foundation on which most sauces are built. Find out the difference between a white stock and a brown stock, a court-bouillon and a fish stock. See how, after simmering and straining, reduction makes what was once water and a few vegetables and meat or fish, into this marvellous, slightly dense liquid, saturated with intense flavours.

As well as the sauces themselves, there is another section in the book with complete recipes which include a sauce in the method. Boeuf Provencal, Boeuf Bourgignon and Boeuf en Daube are famous for their rich, delicious sauces. In seven sub-sections you will find hors d'oeuvres, shellfish, fish, poultry and game, meat, and vegetable dishes with fragrant sauces, and such delicately-flavoured dessert sauces as Vanilla Custard Sauce and Chantilly Cream. Try the sauce suggested, or experiment with the taste buds and make a different one.

Above all, learn the art of making sauces and you will see how, for so little effort, the food you eat can be transformed into something quite wonderful, when it is joined with such a clever partner as a sauce.

BASIC SAUCES

This collection of recipes includes those that are most often found in French cooking. Some are deeply-rooted in traditional French cuisine and have been part of French cooking for centuries. Others are the everyday recipes of the modern-day French cook and, drawing inspiration from other cuisines, are culinary reminders of the cosmopolitan nature of French cuisine.

For ease of reference the sauces are divided into four broad categories: **1**. Composite butters **2**. Sauce stocks and thickenings **3**. Cold sauces **4**. Hot sauces. Some special sauces will be explained in detail in individual recipes.

Composite Butters

Beurre d'escargot

Snail Butter

	00:20 plus standing	00:00
American	**Ingredients**	**Metric/Imperial**
5	Shallots	5
4	Garlic cloves	4
1 cup	Butter, at room temperature	250 g / 8 oz
½	Lemon	½
	Ground fennel	
	Salt and pepper	
3 tbsp	Chopped fresh parsley	3 tbsp

1. Peel and finely chop the shallots. Peel and crush the garlic.
2. Mix together the butter, juice of the ½ lemon, a pinch of fennel, and salt and pepper to taste. Work the butter, adding the garlic, shallots and parsley gradually.
3. Leave to stand for at least 30 minutes before using to stuff the snail shells.
4. Will keep for 10 days in the refrigerator.

Beurre noir
Black Butter

	00:00		00:05

Black butter is the traditional
accompaniment for skate.

American	Ingredients	Metric/Imperial
1 cup	Butter	250 g / 8 oz
5 tbsp	Vinegar	5 tbsp
3 tbsp	Capers	3 tbsp
	Salt and pepper	

1. Heat the butter in a frying pan over a brisk heat until it is a beautiful brown color. Remove from the heat.
2. Gently add the vinegar and capers. Add salt and pepper to taste. Stir to mix.

Beurre de roquefort
Roquefort Butter

	00:10		00:00

American	Ingredients	Metric/Imperial
½ cup	Butter, at room temperature	125 g / 4 oz
2 oz	Roquefort cheese	50 g / 2 oz
1 tsp	Cognac	1 tsp
1 tbsp	Prepared mustard	1 tbsp
	Pepper	

1. Mix the butter and roquefort with a fork, then add the cognac, mustard and pepper to taste. Continue to work the butter with the other ingredients to form a cream.
2. Shape into a roll, wrap in foil and chill until set.
3. You may serve roquefort butter, cut into thin slices, on canapés topped with tomatoes, gherkins or sausage.

Beurre fondu
Drawn or Clarified Butter

	00:05		00:05

American	Ingredients	Metric/Imperial
½ cup	Butter	125 g / 4 oz
½	Lemon (optional)	½
	Salt and pepper	

1. Warm the butter in a bowl placed over a saucepan of boiling water. As soon as the butter has melted, leave it to cool until it is lukewarm. After a moment or two, you will see a whitish deposit forming at the bottom of the bowl: this is the whey.
2. Pour the melted butter very gently into a container so that the whey is left behind. Add the juice of the ½ lemon, if liked, and season to taste.

Beurre d'ail

Garlic Butter

	00:10		00:00

American	Ingredients	Metric/Imperial
3	Garlic cloves	3
½ cup	Butter, at room temperature	125 g / 4 oz
	Salt and pepper	

1. Peel the garlic cloves. Crush them as finely as possible using a mortar and pestle.
2. Blend the garlic with the butter, working with the pestle to obtain an even paste. Add salt and pepper to taste.
3. Shape the garlic butter into a roll and wrap in foil. Chill until firm.
4. The butter will keep, in the refrigerator, for a few days. Cut it into equal slices to serve.

Cook's tip: if you don't like the aftertaste of garlic, chew some fresh parsley at the end of the meal.

Beurre manié

Kneaded Butter

	00:02		00:00

American	Ingredients	Metric/Imperial
1 tbsp	Butter, at room temperature	15 g / ½ oz
1 tbsp	Flour	1 tbsp

1. Mix the butter with the flour, using a fork, to make a paste.
2. Add the kneaded butter in one lump to a boiling sauce, and cook for a further 3-4 minutes, stirring constantly.
3. This quantity will thicken 2 cups [500 ml / ¾ pint].

Beurre maître d'hôtel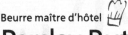

Parsley Butter

	00:15		00:00

American	Ingredients	Metric/Imperial
⅔ cup	Butter, at room temperature	150 g / 5 oz
1 tbsp	Chopped fresh parsley	1 tbsp
½	Lemon	½
	Salt and pepper	

1. Put the butter on a plate. Mash it with a fork, then add the chopped parsley and juice of the ½ lemon. Add salt and pepper to taste. Work the mixture with the fork so as to make it very smooth.
2. Shape the butter into a roll and wrap in foil. Place in the refrigerator, where it will keep for a few days, and chill until firm.
3. When required, cut into equal slices and place on broiled [grilled] meat or fish.

Beurre d'anchois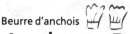

Anchovy Butter

	00:20 plus soaking		00:00

American	Ingredients	Metric/Imperial
½ lb	Salted anchovies	250 g / 8 oz
1	Garlic clove	1
1 cup	Butter, at room temperature	250 g / 8 oz
	Pepper	

1. Put the anchovies into a mixing bowl, cover with water and leave to soak for 2 hours, changing the water several times. Drain.

2. Fillet the anchovies, discarding all skin and bones. Rinse and pat dry with paper towels.

3. Place the anchovies in a mortar. Peel the garlic and add to the mortar. Pound with the pestle to make a fine cream. Gradually add the butter and mix until very smooth. Season lightly with pepper.

4. This anchovy butter, which may be kept at least 3 weeks in the refrigerator, gains in flavour if you make it about 1 hour before using.

5. To serve anchovy butter warm, melt it in a bowl standing in a pan of hot water, whisking it as you do so. To make it finer, you may put it through a very fine strainer to remove fragments of anchovy.

SAUCE STOCKS AND THICKENINGS

Courts-bouillons and concentrates

Courts-bouillons and concentrates form the basis of a large number of fish soups and preparations for fish and shellfish. These are sometimes obtainable ready made, but their flavor does not compare at all with those you can make yourself. The recipe given here for a court-bouillon with vinegar, is extremely good for poaching fat fish (mackerel, tuna, salmon, etc), and that for a fish stock with white wine for lean white fish (sole, bream, etc).

Concentrate (fumet) is prepared from the bones and heads of fish, and is normally used for poaching. Courts-bouillons and concentrates may be kept in the freezer for several months.

Stocks

Stocks made from meat, poultry, fish or just vegetables form the basis for many soups, sauces and stews, and are also used for braising.

White stock, made from white meats (veal or poultry) and flavorings, is used for all dishes based on velouté sauce. Brown stock is made from beef, veal or poultry and flavorings first browned in butter. It is used for making soups, brown sauces, and for moistening stews and braises made with dark meats.

Stocks will keep perfectly for several months in the freezer.

Court-bouillon au vin blanc

Court-Bouillon with White Wine

⊏▭▭➤ 00:15		00:40 ⌐▭▭➤
American	**Ingredients**	**Metric/Imperial**
4	Carrots	4
4	Large onions	4
2	Celery stalks	2
2 quarts	Dry white wine	2 l / 3½ pints
2 quarts	Water	2 l / 3½ pints
1	Fresh thyme sprig	1
1	Bunch of fresh parsley	1
4	Cloves	4
8	Black peppercorns	8
	Salt	

1. Peel the carrots and cut into slices. Peel and thinly slice the onions. Cut the celery into pieces about ¾ in / 2 cm long.

2. Pour the wine into a large saucepan and add the water, carrots, onions, celery, thyme, parsley, cloves, peppercorns and salt to taste. Bring to a boil and simmer for 40 minutes.

3. Leave to cool before straining.

Fonds brun

Brown Stock

This is made from beef, veal, poultry and vegetables, browned in butter before simmering in water with herbs and flavorings. It serves as a base for a large number of sauces.

	00:15	05:00

American	Ingredients	Metric/Imperial
3 tbsp	Butter or oil	3 tbsp
4	Carrots	4
4	Onions	4
1	Garlic clove	1
2 lb	Meaty bones (beef and veal), cut into pieces by the butcher	1 kg / 2 lb
1 lb	Beef for stew	500 g / 1 lb
2 quarts	Water	2 l / 3½ pints
1	Fresh thyme sprig	1
1	Bay leaf	1
2	Fresh parsley sprigs	2
	Salt and pepper	

1. Put the butter or oil into a large roasting pan.

2. Peel the carrots, onions and garlic and cut into large pieces. Place in the roasting pan with the bones and pieces of beef. Brown over a vigorous heat.

3. Add one-quarter of the water and scrape the bottom of the pan with a wooden spatula to detach the sediment.

4. Pour into a stewing pot and add the remaining water, the thyme, bay leaf, parsley, and salt and pepper to taste. Bring to a boil and simmer for 5 hours, skimming the scum from the surface occasionally.

5. Strain the stock through a dampened cloth placed over a large bowl. Twist the corners of the cloth to squeeze out all the liquid. Leave to cool.

6. Store the stock in the freezer if you are not going to use it during the following week.

Fonds blanc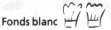

White Stock

🔪	00:30	04:00 🍲
	Makes about 3 quarts (3 l / 5 pints)	

American	Ingredients	Metric/Imperial
	Giblets from 3 chickens or 3 carcasses	
1½ lb	Shoulder of veal	750 g / 1½ lb
2 lb	Shin [knuckle] of veal	1 kg / 2 lb
4 quarts	Cold water	4 l / 7 pints
5	Carrots	5
4	Onions	4
2	Leeks	2
1	Celery stalk	1
1	Fresh thyme sprig	1
1	Bay leaf	1
2	Fresh parsley sprigs	2
	Salt and pepper	

1. Put the giblets into a cooking pot together with the shoulder of veal and the veal shin [knuckle]. Add the cold water. Place the pot over a medium heat and bring to a boil.

2. Meanwhile, peel and slice the carrots and onions. Slice the leeks and celery lengthwise. Skim the stock, then add the vegetables, thyme, bay leaf, parsley, and salt and pepper.

3. Simmer steadily for 3½ hours.

4. Leave the stock to cool until it is lukewarm, then remove any fat from the surface.

5. Strain the stock through a dampened cloth placed over a large bowl. Twist the corners of the cloth so as to squeeze out all the liquid. Cool completely.

6. Remove any remaining fat from the surface of the liquid.

Court-bouillon au vinaigre

Court-Bouillon with Vinegar

🔪	00:15	00:40 🍲

American	Ingredients	Metric/Imperial
4	Carrots	4
4	Large onions	4
2	Celery stalks	2
2	Garlic cloves	2
1¼ - 2 cups	Wine vinegar	300 - 450 ml / ½ - ¾ pint
2 quarts	Water	2 l / 3½ pints
2	Fresh thyme sprigs	2
2	Bay leaves	2
6	Cloves	6
12	Black peppercorns	12
	Salt	

1. Peel and slice the carrots. Peel and thinly slice the onions.

Cut the celery into pieces about ¾ in / 2 cm long. Peel and crush the garlic.

2. Pour the vinegar into a large saucepan and add the water, carrots, onions, celery, thyme, bay leaves, garlic and cloves. Bring to a boil, then add the peppercorns and salt to taste. Simmer for 40 minutes.

3. Leave to cool, then strain.

Sauce espagnole (simplifiée)

Rich Brown Sauce
simplified

	00:20	04:00
	Makes 2 cups [500 ml / ¾ pint]	

American	Ingredients	Metric/Imperial
1 lb	Meaty veal bones, cut into pieces by the butcher	500 g / 1 lb
	Giblets from 2 chickens	
2	Carrots	2
2	Onions	2
1	Leek	1
3	Tomatoes	3
6 tbsp	Lard	75 g / 3 oz
1½ tbsp	Flour	1½ tbsp
1 tbsp	Tomato paste [purée]	1 tbsp
1 quart	Water	1 l / 1¾ pints
2 cups	White wine	500 ml / ¾ pint
	Salt and pepper	
1	Bouquet garni	1

1. Place the bones and giblets in a frying pan and brown.

2. Meanwhile, peel and chop the carrots and onions. Chop the leek. Peel the tomatoes (first plunging them in boiling water for 10 seconds) and cut into large pieces.

3. Melt the lard in a stewpan and add the onions, leek, carrots and tomatoes. Sprinkle with the flour. Mix well, then add the tomato paste diluted in the water, the wine, and salt and pepper to taste. Add the browned bones and giblets and bouquet garni. Bring to a boil. Leave to cook, uncovered, over a gentle heat for about 4 hours. Skim off the scum from the surface from time to time.

4. Strain the sauce. Leave it to cool, then remove any fat from the surface. Keep in the refrigerator until ready to use.

Fumet de poisson

Fish Stock

Fish stock forms the basis for a large number of sauces.

	00:15	01:00
	Makes 2 cups [500 ml / ¾ pint]	

American	Ingredients	Metric/Imperial
2	Large onions	2
2	Shallots	2
2	Large carrots	2
1½ lb	Fish trimmings (heads and bones)	750 g / 1½ lb
1	Bouquet garni	1
½	Lemon	½
1 cup	White wine	250 ml / 8 fl oz
1 quart	Water	1 l / 1¾ pints
	Salt and pepper	

1. Peel and finely chop the onions, shallots and carrots. Roughly crush the fish trimmings.
2. Place the vegetables and fish trimmings in a large saucepan and add the bouquet garni and the ½ lemon cut in two. Pour in the wine and water. Add salt and pepper to taste.
3. Bring to a boil, then reduce the heat and simmer for 1 hour.
4. Strain the stock. It will keep several months in the freezer.

Aspic

This is a clear meat or fish stock which, once it has cooled, solidifies because of the gelatinous substances it contains. Aspics may be obtained naturally or by adding gelatin.

To color aspic
In order to obtain a beautiful amber tint, use caramel or food coloring which you add just before putting the aspic to cool. If you want to amuse your guests, tint it red, or why not green! Use the same colors as for confectionery or cocktails.

To flavor aspic
You may use different wines, spirits or liqueurs which you add, to taste, when the aspic has cooled but not set.

To chop aspic
Turn the firmly-set aspic onto a damp cloth, so that it does not stick, and chop it with a large knife.

To glaze food with aspic
Melt the set aspic without boiling. As soon as it is liquid, remove from the heat and leave to cool, stirring it with a wooden spoon in order to avoid air bubbles. As soon as the aspic begins to take on the consistency of a syrup, ladle it over the very cold food once or twice, putting the food in the refrigerator between the applications.

Gelée de viande

Aspic

This is a recipe for aspic made without gelatin, prepared from naturally gelatinous meat and bones.

00:35   05:00

Makes 2½ quarts [2.5 l / 4½ pints]

American	Ingredients	Metric/Imperial
¼ cup	Butter	50 g / 2 oz
2 lb	Beef for stew (from the leg)	1 kg / 2 lb
1 lb	Shin [knuckle] of veal	500 g / 1 lb
1 lb	Crushed veal and beef bones	500 g / 1 lb
4	Carrots	4
2	Onions	2
1	Large leek	1
1	Celery stalk	1
4 quarts	Water	4 l / 7 pints
2	Boned calf's feet and the crushed bones	2
½ lb	Fresh bacon rind	250 g / 8 oz
1	Bouquet garni	1
	Salt and pepper	
½ lb	Chopped lean beef	250 g / 8 oz
3	Egg whites	3
1 tbsp	Chopped fresh tarragon	1 tbsp
1 tbsp	Chopped fresh chervil or parsley	1 tbsp

1. Heat the butter in a roasting pan and add the leg of beef, shin of veal, cut into pieces, and the crushed bones. Cook until well browned.

2. Meanwhile, peel and chop the carrots and onions. Chop the leek and celery.

3. Place the chopped vegetables in the bottom of a large stewpot together with the meat and place the bones on top. Pour on the water and add the sediment from the roasting pan. Bring to a boil, skimming off the scum that forms on the surface.

4. Add the calf's feet together with the crushed bones, the bacon rind and bouquet garni. Season with salt and pepper and simmer for about 4 hours.

5. Strain the stock. Leave to cool until lukewarm, then skim off the fat from the surface.

6. To clarify the stock, place it in a large saucepan with the chopped beef, the egg whites, the tarragon and the chervil. Blend the whole thoroughly with a wooden spoon. Place the saucepan over the heat and bring the stock to the boil. Turn down the heat and cook at simmering point for 35 minutes.

7. Strain the stock, through a dampened cloth, into a bowl. Squeeze the cloth firmly to extract all the liquid. Cover the bowl with a clean tea towel, leave the liquid to cool, then chill in the refrigerator for 1-2 hours.

8. You may flavor the aspic before it has cooled using fortified wines such as port, sherry, madeira, etc, ⅔ cup [150 ml / ¼ pint] to each quart [1 l / 1¾ pints] aspic, or with dry white wine, 1¼ cups [300 ml / ½ pint] to each 1 quart [1 l / 1¾ pints] aspic.

9. The aspic will keep well in the freezer.

Glace de viande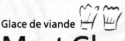

Meat Glaze

	00:30	07:00
	Makes about 1 quart [1 l / 2 pints]	

American	Ingredients	Metric/Imperial
9 lb	Veal bones, sawn into pieces	4 kg / 9 lb
4	Carrots	4
4	Onions	4
2	Garlic cloves	2
1	Celery stalk	1
2 lb	Tomatoes	1 kg / 2 lb
5 quarts	Cold water	5 l / 9 pints
	Bouquet garni	
1 tbsp	Tomato paste [purée]	1 tbsp
	Salt and pepper	

1. Preheat the oven to 500°F / 250°C / Gas Mark 9-10.

2. Place the bones in a roasting pan and bake until browned.

3. Meanwhile, peel and coarsely chop the carrots, onions and garlic. Put the garlic on one side. Chop the celery. Peel the tomatoes (first plunging them in boiling water for 10 seconds) and chop them.

4. Add the chopped carrots, onions and celery to the roasting pan and brown with the bones in the oven.

5. Transfer the browned vegetables and bones to a stewpot. Add the cold water and bring to a boil. Skim off any scum that rises to the surface.

6. Add the garlic, bouquet garni, tomatoes, tomato paste and salt and pepper to taste. Leave to cook for 7 hours over a low heat.

7. Strain the stock. Return it to the pan and boil, skimming frequently, until reduced to the consistency of a dark syrup. Strain again and leave to cool. Keep in the refrigerator.

Gelée de poisson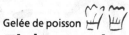

Fish Aspic

This is a fish stock concentrate to which gelatin is added.

00:30 — Makes 2 quarts [2 l / 3½ pints] **00:55**

American	Ingredients	Metric/Imperial
2	Large carrots	2
2	Onions	2
2	Shallots	2
1 lb	Fish bones and trimmings	500 g / 1 lb
2	Fresh parsley sprigs	2
2	Fresh thyme sprigs	2
2	Bay leaves	2
⅔ cup	White wine	150 ml / ¼ pint
2 quarts	Water	2 l / 3½ pints
	Salt and pepper	
¾ lb	Whiting fillets	350 g / 12 oz
1	Bunch of fresh tarragon	1
2	Egg whites	2
2 envelopes	Unflavored gelatin	4 sachets

1. Peel and finely chop the carrots, onions and shallots. Crush the fish bones and trimmings. Place in a large saucepan and add the parsley, thyme, bay leaves, wine, water, and salt and pepper to taste. Cook for 30 minutes over a gentle heat, skimming off any froth that rises to the surface.

2. Meanwhile, chop the whiting fillets and tarragon. Place in a large bowl together with the egg whites and 1 cup [250 ml / 8 fl oz] water. Blend using a whisk.

3. Remove the fish stock from the heat and leave to cool. Strain the stock and add to the whiting mixture.

4. Pour the mixture back into the stewpot and bring to a boil over a gentle heat, stirring constantly with a wooden spoon. Simmer for 25 minutes.

5. Dissolve the gelatin in the remaining water. Stir into the fish stock.

6. Strain the fish stock through a dampened cloth, squeezing the cloth to extract all the liquid. Leave to cool, then place in the refrigerator to chill for 30 minutes before use.

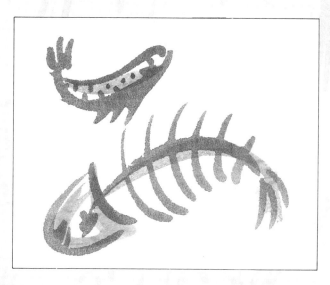

Thickenings

To thicken a sauce or liquid preparation, flour, starch, cream, egg yolk, butter or blood is added.

Liaisons au beurre

Butter Thickenings

These can be difficult to make. To thicken a hot liquid, add cold butter cut into small pieces, whisking rapidly to emulsify it.

Liaisons à la crème

Cream Thickenings

For it to become really silky, cream must lose half its initial volume through evaporation. Thus, if 1 cup [250 ml / 8 fl oz] crème fraîche is added to the same quantity of a sauce or other liquid, the thickening will occur when there is only ½ cup [125 ml / 4 fl oz] left.

To save time, boil the liquid to reduce it, then add the cream, stirring continuously, and leave to reduce once more, until the sauce is of the desired consistency.

Liaisons à la farine ou à la fécule

Flour Thickenings

Dissolve 1 tablespoon flour in 2 tablespoons cold liquid (water, milk, stock, court-bouillon, etc). Add the mixture to 2 cups [500 ml / ¾ pint] sauce to be thickened, stirring continuously until it just returns to a boil and leave to thicken.

Liaisons au jaune d'oeuf

Egg Yolk Thickenings

An egg yolk thickening makes a sauce silky and enriches it. To thicken 2 cups [500 ml / ¾ pint] of sauce, put 2 egg yolks into a bowl and beat them lightly. Add 1 tablespoon of the sauce, mixing continuously with a wooden spoon. Add half the sauce, continuing to stir. Return this mixture to the remainder of the sauce in the saucepan and warm over a gentle heat, stirring constantly, until thickened. Be very careful not to boil the sauce or it will curdle.

Liaisons au sang

Blood Thickenings

Add 2 tablespoons vinegar to animal blood to prevent it congealing. Away from the heat, trickle the blood into the sauce, beating vigorously. Be very careful not to boil.

Marinades

Foods such as meat, game, fish and poultry are often left to soak in a mixture of oil, wine or vinegar, herbs and spices before cooking. This liquid, or marinade, tenderizes and flavors the food.

Marinade crue à l'huile sans vinaigre

Uncooked Marinade without Vinegar

	00:15	00:00
American	**Ingredients**	**Metric/Imperial**
3	Medium-size carrots	3
2	Large onions	2
2	Shallots	2
1	Garlic clove	1
	Celery stalk	
1	Fresh parsley sprig	1
2	Fresh thyme sprigs	2
2	Bay leaves	2
8	Black peppercorns	8
1	Clove	1
	Salt and pepper	
1 quart	Dry white wine	1 l / 1¾ pints
2 cups	Oil	450 ml / ¾ pint
6	Coriander seeds (optional)	6
6	Juniper berries (optional)	6

1. Peel and grate the carrots, onions, shallots and garlic. Grate the celery. Chop the parsley.
2. Put half the grated vegetables into the bottom of a mixing bowl. Add the parsley, thyme, bay leaves, peppercorns and clove.
3. Place the food to be marinated on top. Add salt and pepper to taste. Cover with the remainder of the vegetables. Add the wine and oil.
4. Leave to marinate in a cool place for 12-24 hours, turning the food frequently.

Cook's tip: if you are preparing this marinade for game, add the coriander seeds and crushed juniper berries.

Marinade-express pour grillade

Marinade for Broiled [Grilled] Meat

For small roasts, poultry, fish, etc.

🔪➡ 00:10   00:00 🍲

American	Ingredients	Metric/Imperial
	Pepper	
2	Large onions	2
1	Shallot	1
1	Bunch of fresh parsley	1
1	Garlic clove (optional)	1
1	Fresh thyme sprig	1
1	Bay leaf	1
2	Fresh tarragon sprigs	2
2 cups	Oil	500 ml / ¾ pint
1	Lemon	1

1. Place the meat to be marinated in a shallow dish. Sprinkle pepper over the meat. Do not salt: salt brings out the juices and prevents the meat from being sealed.
2. Peel and grate the onions and shallot. Chop the parsley. Peel and crush the garlic. Scatter the onions, shallot, parsley, garlic, thyme, bay leaf and tarragon over the meat.
3. Cover with the oil and the juice of the lemon. Leave to marinate for 2 hours, turning the meat frequently.

Marinade cuite, au vinaigre

Cooked Marinade with Vinegar

For meat or game.

🔪➡ 00:15   00:30 🍲

American	Ingredients	Metric/Imperial
3	Medium-size carrots	3
2	Large onions	2
2	Shallots	2
1	Garlic clove	1
1	Celery stalk	1
1	Fresh parsley sprig	1
1 tbsp	Oil	1 tbsp
2	Fresh thyme sprigs	2
2	Bay leaves	2
8	Black peppercorns	8
1	Clove	1
1 quart	Dry white or red wine	1 l / 1¾ pints
1¼ cups	Vinegar	300 ml / ½ pint
	Salt and pepper	

1. Peel and slice the carrots, onions, shallots and garlic. Slice the celery. Chop the parsley.

2. Heat a little oil in a saucepan, add the carrots, onions, shallots, celery, garlic, parsley, thyme, bay leaves, peppercorns and clove. Cook over a gentle heat until the vegetables are golden and beginning to soften.

3. Add the wine and vinegar. Bring to a boil and cook over a low heat for 30 minutes. Leave to cool.

4. Place the meat or game in a mixing bowl. Add plenty of salt and pepper. Pour over the cooled marinade and leave to marinate for 24-48 hours in a cool place, but not in the re-frigerator, turning the meat over two or three times.

Roux

A roux — a cooked mixture of butter and flour — is the basis of a large number of preparations and sauces such as white sauce, béchamel sauce, velouté sauce, burgundy sauce, madeira sauce, game sauce and so on.

There are three sorts of roux: white, golden and brown. The color will depend on how long the roux is cooked. It is particularly important, even in the case of white roux, which must not be allowed to color, to make sure that the roux is cooked for long enough to dispel the taste of the raw flour.

Roux blanc

White Roux

 00:00   00:15

Take equal quantities of butter and flour. Melt the butter in a thick-bottomed saucepan. Add the flour all at once and stir vigorously over a very low heat. Continue to cook, stirring constantly, keeping the heat low to prevent the roux from coloring.

Roux blond

Golden Roux

 00:00   00:15

Take equal quantities of butter and flour. Melt the butter in a thick-bottomed saucepan over a medium heat. Add the flour all at once and stir vigorously until the roux turns a golden color.

Roux brun

Brown Roux

 00:00   00:15

Take equal quantities of butter and flour. Melt the butter in a thick-bottomed saucepan over a brisk heat. Add the flour all at once and stir vigorously over a brisk heat until the roux turns an even, light brown color. Take care not to burn the roux, otherwise it will be bitter. A brown roux is used for thickening brown sauces.

COLD SAUCES

Sauce tartare

Tartare Sauce

	00:25	00:00
	Makes 2 cups [500 ml / ¾ pint]	

American	Ingredients	Metric/Imperial
2 cups	Mayonnaise	500 ml / ¾ pint
2 tsp	Vinegar	2 tsp
8	Gherkins	8
1 tsp	Capers	1 tsp
2 tbsp	Chopped mixed fresh chives, tarragon and chervil	2 tbsp
	Salt and pepper	

1. If the mayonnaise is too thick, thin it with a little more vinegar, mixing vigorously.
2. Cut the gherkins into very small cubes. Chop the capers. Add to the mayonnaise with the herbs, and salt and pepper to taste. Mix well.
3. Keep in a cool place.

Mayonnaise

Mayonnaise

	00:20	00:00
	Makes 2 cups [500 ml / ¾ pint]	

American	Ingredients	Metric/Imperial
2	Egg yolks, at room temperature	2
2 cups	Peanut [groundnut] oil	500 ml / ¾ pint
1 tbsp	Strong prepared mustard	1 tbsp
2 tbsp	Lemon juice or vinegar	2 tbsp
	Salt and pepper	

1. For the mayonnaise to be a success, the egg yolks and oil must be at the same temperature. Place the egg yolks and mustard in a large bowl. Add a very small quantity of oil and whisk it in with a balloon whisk or electric beater.
2. Add the remaining oil, very slowly at first. As soon as the sauce is thickening, the oil may be added more rapidly. While adding the oil, whisk or beat constantly. (The mayonnaise may also be made in a blender or food processor.)
3. Add the lemon juice or vinegar, a large pinch of salt, and pepper to taste. Mix well.

Cook's tip: if your mayonnaise separates or curdles, you can save it as follows: put 1 tablespoon of ice water in a clean bowl and gradually whisk or beat in the curdled mayonnaise.

Aïoli
Garlic Mayonnaise

	00:15		00:00
	Makes 1 cup [250 ml / 8 fl oz]		

American	Ingredients	Metric/Imperial
7	Garlic cloves	7
1 cup	Olive oil	250 ml / 8 fl oz
1 - 2	Egg yolks, at room temperature	1 - 2
2 tbsp	Lemon juice	2 tbsp
	Salt and pepper	

1. Peel the garlic and crush in a mortar. Reduce to a cream by adding 1 or 2 tablespoons oil.
2. Add the egg yolks, then the remainder of the oil in a trickle, stirring the sauce continuously to thicken it like a mayonnaise. Add the lemon juice, and salt and pepper to taste.
3. Keep in a cool place.

Cook's tip: garlic mayonnaise is served as a dip with raw and cooked young vegetables, and with cold fish and boiled chicken.

Sauce au basilic (Pesto)
Basil Sauce

	00:15		00:00

American	Ingredients	Metric/Imperial
1	Large bunch of fresh basil	1
4	Garlic cloves	4
1 cup	Olive oil	250 ml / 8 fl oz
	Salt and pepper	

1. Crush the basil leaves and peeled garlic cloves in a mortar.
2. Transfer to a mixing bowl and add the oil, and salt and pepper to taste. Beat with an electric beater or whisk to obtain a green paste or use a blender or food processor.
3. Serve with roasted or broiled [grilled] veal or with pasta and rice and grated parmesan cheese.

Cook's tip: this sauce may be kept for several weeks in the refrigerator.

Sauce vinaigrette

Vinaigrette Dressing

	00:07		00:00
	Makes 4 tablespoons		

American	Ingredients	Metric/Imperial
	Salt and pepper	
1 tbsp	Vinegar	1 tbsp
1 tsp	Prepared mustard	1 tsp
3 tbsp	Oil	3 tbsp
	Chopped mixed fresh herbs (parsley, tarragon, chervil chives) to taste	

1. Dissolve a pinch of salt in the vinegar. Mix in the mustard. Add pepper to taste.
2. Add the oil and chopped herbs. Mix thoroughly.

Sauce vinaigrette à la crème

Vinaigrette Dressing with Cream

	00:05		00:00
	Makes 5 tablespoons		

American	Ingredients	Metric/Imperial
½	Lemon	½
	Salt and pepper	
3 tbsp	Crème fraîche	3 tbsp
	Chopped mixed fresh herbs (parsley, tarragon, chervil chives) to taste	

1. Squeeze the ½ lemon and strain the juice. Dissolve a pinch of salt in the lemon juice.
2. Add the crème fraîche, chopped herbs and pepper to taste. Mix thoroughly.

Rouille
Hot Pepper and Potato Mayonnaise

	00:15		00:00	

American	Ingredients	Metric/Imperial
2	Garlic cloves	2
1	Small hot red pepper [chilli]	1
1	Slice of bread	1
1	Egg yolk	1
⅔ cup	Olive oil	150 ml / ¼ pint
2	Potatoes, boiled in fish soup or stew	2
	Salt and pepper	

1. Peel the garlic. Core the hot pepper and discard the seeds. Place the garlic and pepper in a mortar and crush with a pestle.
2. Soak the bread in a little water and squeeze dry. Add to the mortar and pound to a smooth paste.
3. Add the egg yolk and whisk the sauce, gradually incorporating the oil in a trickle. Mash the potatoes and blend into the sauce. Add salt and pepper to taste.
4. Alternatively, the sauce may be made in a blender or food processor.
5. Hot pepper and potato mayonnaise is very strong and should be used in moderation. It is normally added to fish soups such as bouillabaisse.

Sauce aux noix et au roquefort
Walnut and Roquefort Sauce

	00:10		00:00	

American	Ingredients	Metric/Imperial
3 oz	Roquefort cheese	75 g / 3 oz
⅓ cup	Walnuts	25 g / 1 oz
¼ cup	Olive oil	4 tbsp
1 tsp	Paprika	1 tsp
	Salt and pepper	

1. Crush the roquefort with a fork.
2. Place the walnuts in a blender, food processor or nut grinder. Reduce to a very fine powder.
3. Add the roquefort and then, gradually, the olive oil in a trickle. Continue blending the sauce until all the oil has been used.
4. Add the paprika, and salt and pepper to taste.

Crème fraîche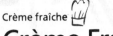

Crème Fraîche

▭▬▬▷	00:05		00:00 🝙
	plus maturing and chilling		

American	Ingredients	Metric/Imperial
1 cup	Heavy [double] cream	300 ml / ½ pint
1 cup	Sour cream	300 ml / ½ pint

1. Combine the creams in a mixing bowl and whisk lightly together.
2. Cover the bowl loosely with plastic wrap and leave in a warm place (at warm room temperature is sufficient) overnight for the culture to develop. (In cold weather, this may take up to 24 hours). At the end of the maturing time, the cream mixture will be thick and subtly tart.
3. Transfer the bowl to the refrigerator and chill for at least 4 hours.
4. Crème fraîche will keep in the refrigerator for 2-3 weeks, and will continue to develop its delicate tartness as it matures.

Cook's tip: crème fraîche can be purchased, or made at home if time permits. If you have no crème fraîche, heavy [double] cream may be used instead for cooked dishes, and sour cream for cold dishes.

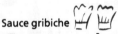

Sauce gribiche

Egg and Herb Sauce

▭▬▬▷	00:20		00:00 🝙

American	Ingredients	Metric/Imperial
4	Hard-cooked eggs	4
1 tbsp	Strong prepared mustard	1 tbsp
1 tbsp	Vinegar	1 tbsp
	Salt and pepper	
1 cup	Peanut [groundnut] oil	250 ml / 8 fl oz
1	Small bunch of fresh parsley	1
3	Fresh tarragon sprigs	3
6	Chive blades	6
1 tbsp	Capers	1 tbsp
1	Shallot	1
1	Small hot red pepper [chilli]	1

1. Shell the eggs and separate the yolks from the whites. Chop the whites. Put the yolks into a mixing bowl and mash them to a paste. Add the mustard, vinegar, and salt and pepper to taste.
2. Pour in the oil gradually in a trickle, beating vigorously with a whisk. Whisk the sauce like a mayonnaise until it is thick.
3. Chop the parsley, tarragon, chives and capers. Peel and chop the shallot. Mix into the sauce with the chopped egg whites. If you like very spicy sauces, add the hot pepper, crushed.

Sauce vinaigrette au lard

Vinaigrette with Bacon

	00:00		00:05

American	Ingredients	Metric/Imperial
6 tbsp	Diced bacon	6 tbsp
2 tbsp	Vinegar	2 tbsp
	Salt and pepper	

1. Cook the diced bacon in a frying pan until crisp and brown and rendered of fat.
2. Pour the bacon and fat over a salad such as dandelion leaves, corn salad [lamb's lettuce] or red cabbage.
3. Pour the vinegar into the still-warm frying pan and stir to mix in the sediment on the bottom and sides of the pan. Pour over the salad. Add salt and pepper to taste and toss.

Sauce rémoulade

Rémoulade Sauce

	00:10		00:00

American	Ingredients	Metric/Imperial
3	Hard-cooked egg yolks	3
1	Egg yolk	1
1 tsp	Prepared mustard	1 tsp
1 cup	Oil	250 ml / 8 fl oz
1 tbsp	Vinegar or lemon juice	1 tbsp
	Salt and pepper	

1. Using a fork, mix the hard-cooked egg yolks with the raw egg yolk and mustard to make a very smooth paste.
2. Pour on the oil gradually, stirring with a wooden spoon until the mixture thickens and has the consistency of mayonnaise.
3. Alternatively, the sauce can be made quickly in a blender or food processor.
4. Add the vinegar or lemon juice, and salt and pepper to taste.

Sauce ravigote

Herb and Mustard Sauce

⊏▭▭▭▭▭ 00:10   00:00 ⊏▭▭

American	Ingredients	Metric/Imperial
1	Hard-cooked egg	1
1 tbsp	Vinegar	1 tbsp
1 tbsp	Prepared mustard	1 tbsp
	Salt and pepper	
3 tbsp	Oil	3 tbsp
1	Garlic clove	1
	Chopped mixed fresh herbs (parsley, tarragon, chervil chives) to taste	

1. Place the egg in a mortar and crush with a pestle. Add the vinegar and mustard. Add salt and pepper to taste.
2. Work with the pestle so that the ingredients are well blended. Pour on the oil gradually, mixing continuously.
3. Peel and crush the garlic. Mix into the sauce. Add the herbs.

Sauce verte

Green Sauce

⊏▭▭▭▭▭ 00:35   00:05 ⊏▭▭

American	Ingredients	Metric/Imperial
2	Egg yolks, at room temperature	2
1 tbsp	Strong prepared mustard	1 tbsp
2 cups	Peanut [groundnut] oil	500 ml / ¾ pint
2 tbsp	Wine vinegar	2 tbsp
	Salt and pepper	
2 oz	Watercress	50 g / 2 oz
2 oz	Spinach	50 g / 2 oz
1	Bunch of fresh chervil	1
1	Bunch of fresh parsley	1
1	Bunch of fresh tarragon	1

1. Put the egg yolks into a mixing bowl and add the mustard. Blend with a whisk, then add the oil gradually in a trickle, whisking continuously.
2. When the mayonnaise is thick, add the vinegar, and salt and pepper to taste.
3. Put the watercress, spinach and herbs into boiling salted water and cook for 5 minutes. Drain and cool under running water. Drain on paper towels.
4. Put the greens into a blender or food processor and blend to a smooth purée.
5. Add the purée to the mayonnaise and mix well.

Sauce raifort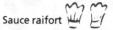

Horseradish Sauce

🔪 00:15   00:00 🍲

American	Ingredients	Metric/Imperial
2 - 3 tbsp	Grated horseradish	2 - 3 tbsp
2 tbsp	White wine vinegar	2 tbsp
2 tsp	Sugar	2 tsp
½ tsp	Mustard powder	½ tsp
½ tsp	Salt	½ tsp
½ tsp	White pepper	½ tsp
1 cup	Chilled crème fraîche	250 ml / 8 fl oz

1. Drain the horseradish, if necessary. Mix the horseradish with the vinegar, sugar, mustard powder, salt and white pepper.
2. Put the crème fraîche into another mixing bowl and whip until thick. Fold in the horseradish mixture. Taste and adjust the seasoning, if necessary.
3. Serve with red meats and broiled [grilled] and smoked fish, especially trout.

Anchoyade

Anchovy and Garlic Purée

🔪 00:05   00:00 🍲
plus soaking
Makes about 1 ½ cups [350 ml / 12 fl oz]

American	Ingredients	Metric/Imperial
16	Salted anchovies	16
1	Shallot	1
2 - 3	Garlic cloves	2 - 3
1 - 2 tbsp	Vinegar	1 - 2 tbsp
1 cup	Olive oil	250 ml / 8 fl oz
	Pepper	

1. Place the anchovies in a bowl and cover with cold water. Let them soak for 2 hours, changing the water several times.
2. Meanwhile, peel and chop the shallot. Peel and crush the garlic. Put the shallot and garlic into a blender or food processor.
3. Drain the anchovies. Fillet them, then rinse with cold water and pat dry on paper towels. Add to the blender.
4. Blend the anchovies, garlic and shallot to a smooth purée.
5. Add half the vinegar, then the oil in a trickle, blending continuously. Add pepper to taste (the sauce must be quite well seasoned) and the remainder of the vinegar.
6. Alternatively, the purée may be made in a mortar and pestle, or using a wooden spoon.
7. Serve the purée as a dip for raw vegetables or spread on warm toast. It also goes very well with broiled [grilled], fried or boiled fish.

HOT SAUCES

Beurre blanc

White Butter Sauce

White butter sauce is a hot emulsified sauce which is often served with fish. It is rather tricky to make, because it is an unstable emulsion which tends to curdle. To make it successfully, add the cold butter cut into small pieces all at once to the boiling wine and shallots, whisking quickly to emulsify it.

	00:20		00:15	

American	Ingredients	Metric/Imperial
12	Shallots	12
⅔ cup	Dry white wine	150 ml / ¼ pint
1 cup	Very cold butter	250 g / 8 oz
1 tbsp	Crème fraîche	1 tbsp
	Salt and pepper	

1. Peel and finely chop the shallots. Place in a saucepan with the wine. Bring to a boil and boil over a moderate heat until the mixture is reduced to one-third.

2. Meanwhile, cut the butter into pieces the size of a walnut.

3. Add the butter all at once to the shallots and cook over a gentle heat, whisking continuously to blend in the butter. Whisk in the crème fraîche.

4. As soon as the sauce has turned white (hence the name of the sauce), add salt and pepper to taste and pour it into a sauceboat.

5. If the sauce has curdled, put 1-2 tablespoons of cold water and 2 teaspoons very cold butter in a saucepan. Place over a gentle heat and gradually incorporate the curdled sauce, whisking vigorously.

Coulis de tomates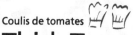

Thick Tomato Sauce

00:20   00:45

American	Ingredients	Metric/Imperial
3 lb	Tomatoes	1.5 kg / 3 lb
2	Garlic clove	2
2	Small onions	2
⅔ cup	Olive oil	150 ml / ¼ pint
1	Bouquet garni	1
5	Fresh basil leaves or	5
1	Fresh tarragon sprig	1
	Salt and pepper	
1 tbsp	Butter	1 tbsp
1 tbsp	Flour	1 tbsp

1. Peel the tomatoes (first plunging them into boiling water for 10 seconds), remove the seeds and chop into large pieces.
2. Peel and chop the garlic and onions. Place in a saucepan with the oil, bouquet garni, basil (or tarragon) and tomatoes. Add salt and pepper to taste. Cover and cook over a gentle heat for 25 minutes.
3. Uncover and cook for a further 10 minutes.
4. Remove the bouquet garni, squeezing it to extract the liquid. Strain the sauce into a clean saucepan. Return to the heat and bring back to a boil.
5. Mix the butter and flour to a smooth paste. Add this kneaded butter (beurre manié) to the boiling sauce and cook for 3-4 minutes, stirring continuously, until thickened.

Sauce aurore

Tomato Cream Sauce

00:05   00:25

American	Ingredients	Metric/Imperial
1	Onion	1
2 tbsp	Butter	25 g / 1 oz
2 tbsp	Flour	2 tbsp
2 cups	Milk	500 ml / ¾ pint
1	Small bouquet garni	1
2 tbsp	Tomato paste [purée]	2 tbsp
2 tbsp	Crème fraîche	2 tbsp
	Grated nutmeg	
	Salt and pepper	

1. Peel and coarsely chop the onion. Melt the butter in a saucepan, add the onion and cook for 5 minutes without browning. Add the flour and cook for 2 minutes, stirring continuously.
2. Remove from the heat and add the cold milk. Bring to a boil, stirring continuously. Add the bouquet garni and leave to simmer for 20 minutes.
3. Strain the sauce and return it to the saucepan. Add the tomato paste and crème fraîche. Add nutmeg, and salt and pepper to taste. Mix well.

Sauce barbecue

Barbecue Sauce

🔪 00:10   00:25 🍲

American	Ingredients	Metric/Imperial
3	Onions	3
5 tbsp	Olive oil	5 tbsp
1 cup	Tomato paste [purée]	250 ml / 8 fl oz
¼ cup	Vinegar (preferably cider vinegar)	4 tbsp
⅔ cup	White wine or stock	150 ml / ¼ pint
⅔ cup	Worcestershire sauce	150 ml / ¼ pint
3	Fresh thyme sprigs	3
1	Bay leaf	1
2	Garlic cloves	2
¼ cup	Honey	4 tbsp
1 tsp	Prepared mustard	1 tsp
	Salt and pepper	
	Tabasco sauce	

1. Peel and finely chop the onions. Heat the oil in a heavy saucepan, add the onions and soften over a moderate heat.
2. When the onions begin to brown, add the tomato paste mixed with the vinegar. Bring to a boil.
3. Add the wine, worcestershire sauce, thyme, bay leaf, peeled and crushed garlic, honey and mustard. Leave to simmer uncovered for 12 minutes.
4. Add salt and pepper and 2 or 3 drops of tabasco sauce.

Sauce chaud-froid

White Coating Sauce

This sauce is used to coat cooked poultry, fish or eggs.

🔪 01:00   03:30 🍲

American	Ingredients	Metric/Imperial
1½ lb	Shin [knuckle] of veal	750 g / 1½ lb
3	Carrots	3
3	Onions	3
3	Leeks	3
1	Celery stalk	1
3 quarts	Cold water	3 l / 5 pints
	Giblets from 3 chickens	
1	Bouquet garni	1
2 - 3	Cloves	2 - 3
	Salt and pepper	
16	Egg yolks	16
⅔ cup	Crème fraîche	150 ml / ¼ pint
1½ cups	Very fresh butter	350 g / 12 oz

1. Soak the veal in cold water for 3 hours.
2. Meanwhile, peel the carrots and onions and slice thinly. Slice the leeks and celery.
3. Drain the veal and put it in a large saucepan. Add the

measured cold water, chicken giblets, sliced vegetables, bouquet garni, cloves, and salt and pepper to taste. Cook for 3 hours over a low heat, skimming off the scum from the surface from time to time.

4. Strain the stock through a dampened cloth placed over another large saucepan. Twist the corners of the cloth to squeeze out all the liquid. Boil to reduce over a low heat until only 1 quart [1 l / 1¾ pints] remains.

5. Beat the egg yolks with the crème fraîche in a cold bowl. Gradually add the stock, whisking continuously. Finally add the butter, cut into small pieces, stirring well. Taste and adjust the seasoning.

6. Place the food to be coated on a rack over a tray. Spoon over the sauce several times. Leave to cool completely before serving.

Sauce bordelaise

Bordelaise Sauce

This sauce usually accompanies steak. The traditional recipe is a very complicated brown sauce enriched with poached beef marrow, but the one given here is a simplified version which is quicker and less expensive.

00:10   00:15 to 00:20

American	Ingredients	Metric/Imperial
5	Shallots	5
1¼ cups	Red wine	30 ml / ½ pint
1	Fresh thyme sprig	1
1	Bay leaf	1
	Salt and pepper	
¼ cup	Butter	50 g / 2 oz
1 tbsp	Flour	1 tbsp
1¼ cups	Beef stock	300 ml / ½ pint
2 oz	Beef marrow	50 g / 2 oz
2 - 3 tbsp	Meat juice	2 - 3 tbsp
1	Small bunch of fresh parsley	1

1. Peel and chop the shallots and place in a saucepan. Add the red wine, thyme, bay leaf and a pinch of salt. Bring to a boil and reduce by half.

2. Meanwhile, melt 1 tablespoon [15 g / ½ oz] butter in another saucepan. Add the flour and cook, stirring, until the roux has browned. Add the stock and salt and pepper to taste, stirring well. Cook over a low heat for 15 minutes, stirring frequently.

3. Dice the marrow. Poach for 5 minutes in boiling water, then drain.

4. Remove the thyme and bay leaf from the wine reduction. Add the wine to the other saucepan. Add the marrow cubes, adjust the seasoning and leave to simmer for 2-3 minutes.

5. Add the meat juice. Remove from the heat and add the remainder of the butter and the chopped parsley, stirring continuously.

6. If you do not use the sauce immediately, keep it warm in a bowl standing over a pan of hot water.

Sauce bourguignonne

Burgundy Sauce

🔪 00:00   00:30 🍳

American	Ingredients	Metric/Imperial
¼ lb	Mushrooms	125 g / 4 oz
3 - 4	Shallots	3 - 4
¼ lb	Fresh pork sides [belly pork]	125 g / 4 oz
6 tbsp	Butter	75 g / 3 oz
1 quart	Red wine	1 l / 1¾ pints
1	Bouquet garni	1
	Salt and pepper	
2 tbsp	Flour	25 g / 1 oz

1. Chop the mushrooms. Peel and chop the shallots. Dice the pork very finely.
2. Melt 2 tablespoons [25 g / 1 oz] butter in a saucepan, add the mushrooms and pork and cook until lightly browned.
3. Add the red wine, shallots, bouquet garni, and salt and pepper to taste. Bring to a boil and reduce by half.
4. Remove the bouquet garni. Blend the flour and 2 tablespoons [25 g / 1 oz] butter to a paste (beurre-manié) and add to the sauce, stirring it with a whisk. Boil for 3-4 minutes until thickened, then add the remainder of the butter and whisk it in.

Sauce diable

Devil Sauce

🔪 00:15   00:45 🍳

American	Ingredients	Metric/Imperial
4	Shallots	4
2 cups	White wine	450 ml / ¾ pint
5 tbsp	Vinegar	5 tbsp
1	Fresh thyme sprig	1
1	Bay leaf	1
	Salt and pepper	
¼ cup	Butter	50 g / 2 oz
3 tbsp	Flour	25 g / 1 oz
2 cups	Beef stock	500 ml / ¾ pint
1	Bunch of fresh parsley	1

1. Peel and chop the shallots. Place them in a saucepan with the wine, vinegar, thyme sprig, bay leaf, and salt and pepper to taste. Boil until reduced to ½ cup [125 ml / 4 fl oz] liquid.
2. Meanwhile, melt 2 tablespoons [25 g / 1 oz] butter in a heavy saucepan over a medium heat. Add the flour and stir with a wooden spoon until the roux turns light brown in color. Add pepper to taste and pour on the stock, stirring constantly. Cook gently for 15 minutes, stirring from time to time.
3. Add the reduced wine mixture to the sauce and stir. Leave to cook over a low heat for about 5 minutes longer.
4. Chop the parsley. Remove the saucepan from the heat. Discard the thyme sprig and bay leaf. Swirl in the rest of the butter and the chopped parsley. Serve hot.

Sauce béchamel
Béchamel Sauce

🔪 00:05 　　　　　 00:45 🍲

American	Ingredients	Metric/Imperial
5 tbsp	Butter	5 tbsp
5 tbsp	Flour	50 g / 2 oz
1 quart	Milk	1 l / 1¾ pints
	Grated nutmeg	
	Salt and pepper	
1	Medium-size onion (optional)	1
1	Clove	1
1	Small bouquet garni (optional)	1

1. Melt the butter in a heavy saucepan. Add the flour and stir vigorously with a wooden spoon until the butter completely absorbs the flour. Cook, stirring, for 2-3 minutes.
2. Remove from the heat and gradually pour in the milk, stirring continuously. Return the saucepan to the heat and bring slowly to a boil, stirring. Cook over a gentle heat for 10 minutes. Add nutmeg, salt and pepper to taste. The sauce is now ready to serve.
3. If liked, peel and halve the onion and stud with the clove. Add to the sauce with the bouquet garni and leave to simmer for a further 25-30 minutes, stirring frequently. Strain through a fine sieve.
4. This sauce keeps very well in the refrigerator. Cover it with a sheet of plastic wrap to prevent a skin forming.

Sauce brune

Brown Sauce

	00:15	00:35

American	Ingredients	Metric/Imperial
3	Onions	3
5 oz	Bacon	150 g / 5 oz
6 tbsp	Butter	75 g / 3 oz
6 tbsp	Flour	75 g / 3 oz
1 quart	Beef stock	1 l / 1¾ pints
	Salt and pepper	
1	Bouquet garni	1

1. Peel and thinly slice the onions. Cut the bacon into small cubes. Melt the butter in a saucepan, add the onions and bacon and cook over a very gentle heat until lightly browned.
2. Add the flour and stir to mix. Cook, stirring, until the mixture becomes light brown.
3. Add the stock and bring to a boil, stirring well. Add salt and pepper to taste. Add the bouquet garni. Cook for 20 minutes over a very gentle heat.
4. Taste and adjust the seasoning, then boil the sauce to reduce it for a further 10 minutes.
5. Before serving skim off any fat or scum from the surface and discard the bouquet garni.

Sauce blanche

White Sauce

White sauce is prepared like béchamel, but the milk is replaced by the same quantity of water or stock.

Sauce béarnaise

Béarnaise Sauce

This sauce can be difficult to make. The secret of success is to stir it continuously during preparation. Also, the butter must be fresh and of excellent quality.

	00:10	00:20

American	Ingredients	Metric/Imperial
2	Shallots	2
2 - 3	Fresh tarragon sprigs	2 - 3
2	Fresh chervil or parsley sprigs	2
¾ cup	Butter	175 g / 6 oz
1 tbsp	Oil	1 tbsp
⅔ cup	Vinegar	150 ml / ¼ pint
	Salt and pepper	
3	Egg yolks, at room temperature	3
2 tbsp	Cold water	2 tbsp

1. Peel and finely chop the shallots. Chop the tarragon and chervil.

2. Heat 1 tablespoon [15 g / ½ oz] butter and the oil in a saucepan and add the shallots, half the chopped tarragon and chervil and the vinegar. Add pepper to taste. Place over a gentle heat and leave to reduce for 20 minutes until only 1 tablespoon of the vinegar remains.

3. Meanwhile, heat the remaining butter in a bowl standing over a pan of hot water. When the butter has melted, leave it to cool until it is lukewarm. After a moment or two, a whitish deposit will appear and fall to the bottom of the pan. Pour the melted butter into a bowl, leaving the sediment behind.

4. Place the egg yolks in a bowl over the pan of hot water, add the vinegar reduction and whisk well. Gradually incorporate the water, and salt and pepper to taste. Continue to whisk vigorously until the mixture becomes creamy. Remove from the heat and, continuing to whisk, add the melted butter in a thin trickle. When all the butter has been incorporated, you will have a very smooth sauce.

5. Strain the sauce, if liked, then add the remaining tarragon and chervil.

6. If you do not use the sauce immediately, place the bowl over a pan of hot, but not boiling, water.

Sauce choron

Tomato Béarnaise Sauce

	00:20		00:30	

American	Ingredients	Metric/Imperial
2 lb	Tomatoes	1 kg / 2 lb
1 quantity	Béarnaise sauce	1 quantity

1. Cut the tomatoes into large pieces and place in a heavy saucepan. Cook over a medium heat until thick and well reduced.

2. Strain through a food mill or conical strainer: you should obtain a very thick purée.

3. Mix the tomato purée with the béarnaise sauce.

Sauce hollandaise

Hollandaise Sauce

	00:05	00:15
American	**Ingredients**	**Metric/Imperial**
1 ½ cups	Butter	350 g / 12 oz
4	Egg yolks, at room temperature	4
2 tsp	Cold water	2 tsp
½ tsp	Salt	½ tsp

1. Work the butter on a plate with a fork to soften it.
2. Place a saucepan half filled with water over the heat (choose a saucepan large enough for a large bowl to fit over it) and bring to a boil.
3. Put into a large bowl the egg yolks, cold water and salt. Place the bowl on the saucepan of boiling water and stir vigorously with a whisk.
4. As soon as the eggs begin to thicken over the heat, remove the bowl from the heat and add the softened butter in small pieces, whisking continuously. It is very important to continue whisking at this stage to achieve a very smooth, pale-yellow sauce. If you do not want to serve it immediately, place the bowl of hollandaise sauce back over the pan of hot but not boiling water, off the heat, to keep warm.

Cook's tip: when you incorporate the butter, if the sauce becomes too thick, immediately add a few more drops of cold water to thin it out.

Sauce financière (simplifiée)

Madeira Mushroom Sauce (simplified)

	00:30	00:30
American	**Ingredients**	**Metric/Imperial**
14 oz	Small mushrooms	400 g / 14 oz
	Lemon juice	
6 tbsp	Butter	75 g / 3 oz
6 tbsp	Flour	75 g / 3 oz
1 quart	Chicken stock	1 l / 1¾ pints
	Salt and pepper	
1 - 2 tbsp	Truffle peelings	1 - 2 tbsp
1¼ cups	Madeira	300 ml / ½ pint

1. Clean the mushrooms and sprinkle with lemon juice to prevent them discoloring.
2. Melt the butter in a heavy saucepan over medium heat, add the flour and stir vigorously until the roux turns a golden color.
3. Add the chicken stock, stirring well. Add salt and pepper to taste. Add the whole mushrooms. Leave to cook over a low heat for 25 minutes.
4. About 5 minutes before serving, add the truffle peelings and madeira.

Sauce mornay
Cheese Sauce

	00:05			00:15

American	Ingredients	Metric/Imperial
6 tbsp	Butter	75 g / 3 oz
6 tbsp	Flour	75 g / 3 oz
1 quart	Milk	900 ml / 1 ½ pints
	Grated nutmeg	
	Salt and pepper	
1 ¼ cups	Grated gruyère cheese	150 g / 5 oz

1. Melt the butter in a heavy saucepan. Add the flour and cook, stirring with a wooden spoon, for 2-3 minutes. Remove from the heat and add the milk, stirring well. Return to the heat and cook, stirring, until the sauce has thickened. Leave to cook for about 10 minutes. Add nutmeg, salt and pepper to taste.
2. Add the cheese gradually, continuing to stir the sauce so that the cheese will melt evenly as it blends in.

Sauce Grand Veneur (simplifiée)
Grand Veneur Sauce
(simplified)

	00:20			02:00

American	Ingredients	Metric/Imperial
1	Garlic clove	1
2	Carrots	2
2	Onions	2
2	Shallots	2
¼ cup	Oil	4 tbsp
1 ¼ tbsp	Flour	1 ¼ tbsp
1 tbsp	Cognac	1 tbsp
⅔ cup	Vinegar	150 ml / ¼ pint
2 cups	Beef stock	500 ml / ¾ pint
2 cups	Red wine which was used for marinating game	500 ml / ¾ pint
	Salt and pepper	
6 tbsp	Red currant jelly	6 tbsp

1. Peel and crush the garlic. Peel the carrots, onions and shallots and cut into small cubes. Heat the oil in a frying pan, add the carrots, onions and shallots and cook over a very brisk heat, stirring, until lightly browned.
2. Sprinkle with the flour, stir well and leave to brown. Add the cognac, vinegar, beef stock, red wine which was used in the marinade and garlic. Bring to a boil, then season to taste with salt and pepper. Cook for 2 hours over a very gentle heat.
3. Place the red currant jelly in a saucepan and melt it over a very gentle heat. Cook until caramelized. Add to the sauce and cook for a further 5 minutes.
4. Strain the sauce into a clean saucepan, then boil to reduce it further until it has a silky consistency, skimming if necessary.

Sauce mousseline

Whipped Cream Sauce

	00:00		00:10

American	Ingredients	Metric/Imperial
6 tbsp	Very fresh butter	75 g / 3 oz
½ cup	Crème fraîche	125 ml / 4 fl oz
⅔ cup	Vinegar	150 ml / ¼ pint
6	Black peppercorns	6
2	Egg yolks	2

1. Work the butter on a plate with a fork to soften it.
2. Pour the crème fraîche into an ice cold bowl. Whip until thick. Set aside.
3. Place the vinegar and peppercorns in a saucepan and cook over a low heat until only 1 tablespoon of liquid remains.
4. Remove from heat. Remove the peppercorns and beat in the egg yolks. As soon as the eggs begin to thicken, add the softened butter in small pieces, beating continuously.
5. Add the whipped cream and beat well. Serve the sauce with baked fish, or with lightly cooked young vegetables.

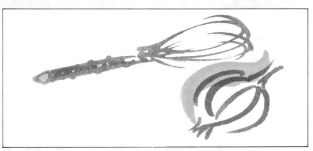

Sauce matelote

Sailor's Sauce

	00:10		00:35

American	Ingredients	Metric/Imperial
1	Garlic clove	1
1	Shallot	1
⅔ cup	Red wine	150 ml / ¼ pint
1¼ cups	Water	300 ml / ½ pint
1	Bouquet garni	1
	Salt and pepper	
6 tbsp	Butter	75 g / 3 oz
2 tbsp	Flour	25 g / 1 oz
2 tbsp	Cognac	2 tbsp

1. Peel and chop the garlic and shallot. Place in a saucepan with the wine, water, bouquet garni, and salt and pepper to taste. Boil to reduce to ⅔ cup [150 ml / ¼ pint] liquid.
2. Melt 2 tablespoons [25 g / 1 oz] butter in another saucepan over a very brisk heat. Add the flour and stir vigorously until the roux has browned. Add the reduced wine mixture and stir well to mix. Cook for a further 10 minutes.
3. Discard the bouquet garni. Add the cognac and remaining butter. Stir to mix and serve hot.

Sauce au kari

Curry Sauce

| | 00:20 | 00:40 to 00:50 |

American	Ingredients	Metric/Imperial
4	Medium-size onions	4
1 tbsp	Oil	1 tbsp
1 - 2 tbsp	Curry powder	1 - 2 tbsp
2 cups	Dry white wine	450 ml / ¾ pint
¼ cup	Water	4 tbsp
	Salt	
1 tbsp	Butter	1 tbsp
1 tbsp	Flour	1 tbsp
1 cup	Crème fraîche	250 ml / 8 fl oz

1. Peel and thinly slice the onions. Heat the oil in a saucepan, add the onions and cook gently until softened without browning (at least 25 minutes).
2. Sprinkle with 1 tablespoon curry powder and stir well. Pour on the wine and water. Add salt to taste but no pepper. Simmer for 20 minutes, stirring occasionally.
3. Purée the sauce in a blender or food processor, then return it to the saucepan. Add the second tablespoon of curry powder, if liked, and simmer for a further 5 minutes.
4. Meanwhile, mix the butter and flour to a paste (beurre manié) with a fork, then divide into small pieces. Add to the sauce and whisk to thicken.
5. Add the crème fraîche and heat through, stirring frequently. If the sauce is too thick, thin it out with a little boiling water.

Cook's tip: if this sauce is to be served with fish, substitute fish stock for the wine and water.

Sauce miroton

Brown Onion Sauce

| | 00:15 | 00:40 |

American	Ingredients	Metric/Imperial
4	Large onions	4
¼ cup	Lard	50 g / 2 oz
2 tbsp	Flour	25 g / 1 oz
2 tbsp	Tomato paste [purée]	2 tbsp
2½ cups	Beef stock	600 ml / 1 pint
	Salt and pepper	
2 tsp	Vinegar	2 tsp

1. Peel and finely chop the onions. Melt the lard in a saucepan, add the onions and brown slightly. Add the flour and stir vigorously until it browns.
2. Mix the tomato paste with the stock and add to the pan, stirring well. Add salt and pepper to taste. Leave to cook for a further 10 minutes, stirring frequently.
3. Stir in the vinegar and serve hot.

Sauce moutarde

Mustard Sauce

	00:10	00:10 to 00:12

American	Ingredients	Metric/Imperial
2	Shallots	2
¼ cup	Butter	50 g / 2 oz
2 tbsp	Flour	3 tbsp
1 ½ cups	Crème fraîche	350 ml / 12 fl oz
1 tbsp	Strong prepared mustard	1 tbsp
	Salt and pepper	
1	Egg yolk	1
	Lemon juice	

1. Peel and finely chop the shallots. Melt 2 tablespoons [25 g / 1 oz] butter in a saucepan, add the shallots and cook until soft but not brown.

2. Add the remainder of butter and, as soon as it has melted, add the flour. Cook for 2 minutes, stirring, then stir in the crème fraîche. Cook until the mixture thickens, stirring constantly.

3. Add the mustard. Add salt and pepper to taste. The sauce should be very spicy.

4. Lightly beat the egg yolk with a few drops of lemon juice and 1 tablespoon of the sauce. Add this mixture to the hot (but not boiling) sauce, stirring well. If the sauce seems too thick, thin it with a little boiling water added in small spoonfuls.

5. Serve with fish. The sauce may also be flavored with chopped herbs.

Sauce veloutée

Velouté Sauce

	00:15	00:03
	Makes 2 cups [500 ml / ¾ pint]	

American	Ingredients	Metric/Imperial
2 tbsp	Butter	25 g / 1 oz
1 tbsp	Flour	1 tbsp
⅔ cup	Cooking liquid from the dish to be accompanied	150 ml / ¼ pint
2	Egg yolks	2
½ cup	Crème fraîche	125 ml / 4 fl oz
	Lemon juice	
	Salt and pepper	

1. Melt the butter in a saucepan, add the flour and cook for 2 minutes, stirring.

2. Pour in the cooking liquid, stirring well. Bring to a boil and simmer for 1 minute over a gentle heat.

3. Leave to cool a little, then add the egg yolks mixed with the crème fraîche. Add a few drops of lemon juice, and salt and pepper to taste. Cook, stirring, until thick and smooth. Do not allow to boil.

Sauce Nantua

Crayfish Sauce

	01:00		00:45	

American	Ingredients	Metric/Imperial
2	Small onions	2
1	Shallot	1
10 tbsp	Butter	150 g / 5 oz
3 tbsp	Flour	3 tbsp
3 cups	Milk	750 ml / 1 ¼ pints
5	Fresh parsley sprigs	5
1	Fresh thyme sprig	1
	Grated nutmeg	
	Salt and pepper	
1	Small carrot	1
1	Small garlic clove	1
1	Small bouquet garni	1
8 - 10	Crayfish	8 - 10
1 tbsp	Vinegar	1 tbsp
1 cup	Crème fraîche	250 ml / 8 fl oz

1. Peel and finely chop one onion and the shallot. Melt 2 tablespoons [25 g / 1 oz] butter in a saucepan, add the onion and shallot and cook over a very moderate heat without browning. Sprinkle with the flour, stirring, and leave to cook for 2 minutes.

2. Pour on the milk, stirring well. Bring to a boil, stirring, then add the parsley, thyme and a pinch of nutmeg. Add salt and pepper to taste. Simmer over a very low heat until the sauce has reduced by about one-third.

3. Strain the sauce into a bowl, pressing down firmly on the solids to extract all the liquid from them. Cover the bowl with wax [greaseproof] paper or polyurethane film to prevent a skin from forming, and set aside.

4. Peel and thinly slice the remaining onion. Peel and grate the carrot. Peel and crush the garlic. Heat 2 tablespoons [25 g / 1 oz] butter in a frying pan, add the carrot, sliced onion, garlic and bouquet garni. Add pepper to taste and cook over a gentle heat until lightly browned.

5. Meanwhile, prepare the crayfish. Take them with one hand by the head, lowering the pincers forwards. With the other hand, grasp the central tail fin between the thumb and index finger. Twist and pull: a small black intestine will come out with the fin. Remove it. Pat the crayfish dry with paper towels.

6. Add the vinegar to the frying pan. Toss the crayfish into the pan and cook briskly until they turn red. Reduce the heat, cover and leave to cook for 8-10 minutes.

7. Remove the pan from the heat. Leave to cool slightly, then peel the crayfish tails. Set them aside, and reserve the shells, heads and pincers. Crush the shells, heads and pincers in a mortar. Add the remainder of the butter and the vegetable mixture in the frying pan and knead it in with the pestle. Press the butter through a sieve with the pestle.

8. Uncover the white sauce, place it in a saucepan and warm it over a gentle heat. Add the crème fraîche and continue cooking for 2-3 minutes, stirring continuously.

9. Put the pan over another pan containing hot water. Incorporate the crayfish butter in small pieces. Add the crayfish tails.

10. Serve with eggs, fish and shellfish.

Sauce Périgueux

Madeira Truffle Sauce

Before making this sauce you will need to cook the madeira sauce and meat glaze.

🔪	00:00	01:00 🥘
American	**Ingredients**	**Metric/Imperial**
2 cups	White wine	500 ml / ¾ pint
1-2 tbsp	Truffle peelings	1-2 tbsp
2 cups	Madeira sauce (see page 47)	500 ml / ¾ pint
1 cup	Meat glaze (see page 18)	250 ml / 8 fl oz
1 tbsp	Cornstarch [cornflour]	1 tbsp
2 tbsp	Water	2 tbsp
6 tbsp	Butter	75 g / 3 oz

1. Place the wine, truffle peelings and madeira sauce in a heavy saucepan. Cover and simmer for 20 minutes.
2. Add the meat glaze and simmer for a further 20 minutes.
3. Dissolve the cornstarch in the water. Add to the sauce, stirring well, and cook for 5 minutes.
4. Add the butter gradually, stirring constantly. Cover the chosen food with the sauce just before serving.

Sauce saupiquet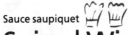

Spiced Wine Sauce

In the Middle Ages, saupiquet was simply a wine sauce thickened with toast which was served with roasted rabbit. Today it is served with chicken, veal and lamb.

🔪	00:10	00:35 🥘
American	**Ingredients**	**Metric/Imperial**
6	Shallots	6
8	Black peppercorns	8
⅔ cup	Wine vinegar	150 ml / ¼ pint
7	Juniper berries	7
¼ cup	Butter	50 g / 2 oz
1½ tbsp	Flour	1½ tbsp
1 cup	Beef stock	250 ml / 8 fl oz
1 cup	White wine	250 ml / 8 fl oz
⅔ cup	Crème fraîche	150 ml / ¼ pint
	Salt and pepper	

1. Peel and chop the shallots. Crush the peppercorns in a mortar. Place the shallots and peppercorns in a saucepan with the vinegar and juniper berries. Bring to a boil, then leave to reduce until the vinegar has completely evaporated.
2. Meanwhile, melt 2 tablespoons [25 g / 1 oz] butter in a heavy saucepan, add the flour and stir vigorously with a wooden spoon over a low heat. Add the stock and wine, stirring well. Leave to cook for 15 minutes, stirring frequently.
3. Add the shallot mixture to the sauce. Leave to cook for a further 15 minutes over a gentle heat, continuing to stir

frequently. Strain the sauce.

4. Add the crème fraîche to the strained pepper sauce, and then the remainder of the butter. Add salt and pepper to taste. Serve very hot.

Sauce madère (recette moderne)

Madeira Sauce
(modern recipe)

00:15		00:40

American	Ingredients	Metric/Imperial
½ lb	Beef for stew	250 g / 8 oz
3	Shallots	3
2	Small onions	2
½ cup	Butter	125 g / 4 oz
1	Fresh thyme sprig	1
1	Bay leaf	1
	Few fresh parsley sprigs	
3 tbsp	Cognac	3 tbsp
⅔ cup	Dry madeira	150 ml / ¼ pint
⅔ cup	Water	150 ml / ¼ pint
	Salt and pepper	
1 tbsp	Flour	1 tbsp
	Grated nutmeg	

1. Cut the meat into very small pieces. Peel and chop the shallots and onions.

2. Heat 1 tablespoon butter [15 g / ½ oz] in a saucepan, add the beef, shallots, onions, thyme, bay leaf and parsley and cook over a medium heat until the meat is browned. Sprinkle with the cognac, then pour on the madeira and water. Add salt and pepper to taste. Cover and simmer for 25-30 minutes.

3. Strain the sauce, pressing the solids to extract the liquid.

4. Melt 1 tablespoon [15 g / ½ oz] butter in the cleaned saucepan, add the flour and leave to brown, stirring continuously. Add the strained sauce, stirring, and bring to a boil. This sauce must be creamy but not thick so do not let it cook too long. Thin it out with a little boiling water if necessary.

5. Adjust the seasoning, and add a pinch of grated nutmeg. Remove from the heat and add the remaining butter in small pieces, whisking to blend it in.

Sauce poivrade

Game Sauce

This sauce is usually served with game.

🔪 00:20   00:50 🥘

American	Ingredients	Metric/Imperial
4	Carrots	4
4	Medium-size onions	4
3	Shallots	3
1	Leek, white part only	1
6 tbsp	Oil	6 tbsp
	Game trimmings (all the bits removed before cooking)	
1¼ lb	Flour	1¼ tbsp
2 cups	Wine from the game marinade or dry white wine	500 ml / ¾ pint
⅔ cup	Wine vinegar	150 ml / ¼ pint
	Salt and pepper	
1	Bouquet garni	1
6-7	Black peppercorns	6-7
1 tbsp	Red currant jelly	1 tbsp
¼ cup	Butter	50 g / 2 oz

1. Peel and chop the carrots, onions and shallots. Chop the leek. Heat the oil in a frying pan, add the chopped vegetables and game trimmings and cook until browned. Add the flour and stir well.

2. Add the wine and vinegar. Season to taste with salt and pepper. Add the bouquet garni, crushed peppercorns and red currant jelly. Cook for 5 minutes over a very low heat, stirring frequently.

3. Strain the sauce. Swirl in the butter.

Sauce poulette

Chicken Cream Sauce with Onions

⊏▭ 00:10		00:20 ⊂▱
American	**Ingredients**	**Metric/Imperial**
5 oz	Pearl [button] onions	150 g / 5 oz
½ cup	Butter	125 g / 4 oz
2 tbsp	Flour	2 tbsp
1¾ cups	Chicken stock	400 ml / 14 fl oz
	Salt and pepper	
½	Lemon	½
2	Egg yolks	2

1. Peel the onions. Set aside. Melt ¼ cup [50 g / 2 oz] butter in a heavy saucepan. Add the flour and stir well, then add the chicken stock. Stir over a gentle heat until boiling.
2. Place the onions in the saucepan. Add salt and pepper to taste. Simmer for 15 minutes over a very gentle heat.
3. About 5 minutes before cooking is completed, add the juice of the ½ lemon and bring back to a boil.
4. Mix the egg yolks with the remaining butter to obtain a cream. Add 1 tablespoon of the sauce, whisking continuously. Add the remaining sauce, continuing to stir. Serve hot.

Sauce suprême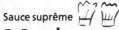

Mushroom and Chicken Cream Sauce

⊏▭ 00:30		00:30 ⊂▱
American	**Ingredients**	**Metric/Imperial**
5 oz	Mushrooms	150 g / 5 oz
½	Lemon	½
¼ cup	Butter	50 g / 2 oz
¼ cup	Flour	50 g / 2 oz
5 cups	Chicken stock	1.2 l / 2 pints
½ cup	Crème fraîche	125 ml / 4 fl oz
2	Egg yolks	2
	Salt and pepper	

1. Cut the mushrooms into small cubes. Place them in a bowl of water to which the juice of ½ lemon has been added to prevent them from discoloring.
2. Melt the butter in a heavy saucepan. Add the flour and stir vigorously over a low heat. Stir in the chicken stock. Add the drained mushrooms. Leave to cook for 30 minutes over a low heat.
3. Add the crème fraîche and stir for a few minutes over a gentle heat.
4. Lightly beat the egg yolks in a mixing bowl. Add 2 tablespoons of the sauce and stir well. Gradually stir in the remaining sauce. Add salt and pepper to taste.

Sauce normande

Normande Sauce

🔪 00:15		00:15 🍲

American	Ingredients	Metric/Imperial
3 tbsp	Butter	40 g / 1½ oz
3 tbsp	Flour	40 g / 1½ oz
2 cups	Fish stock	500 ml / ¾ pint
	Salt and pepper	
1	Egg yolk	1
½ cup	Crème fraîche	125 ml / 4 fl oz

1. Melt the butter in a heavy saucepan. Sprinkle on the flour and cook, stirring, for 2-3 minutes.
2. Add the fish stock all at once, stirring continuously. Cook the sauce, stirring frequently, for 10 minutes.
3. Add salt and pepper to taste. Lightly beat the egg yolk with the crème fraîche. Add to the sauce and stir well. Do not allow the sauce to boil once you have added the egg yolk because it could curdle.

Sauce riche

Rich Sauce

This is a variation of mushroom and chicken cream sauce (see page 49). To the diced mushrooms add ⅔ cup [150ml/¼pint] cognac, 1-2 tablespoons truffle peelings and, to be completely traditional, 1 tablespoon lobster butter.

Sauce zingara

Brown Julienne Sauce

This sauce is served with all roast meats.

🔪 00:30	00:25 to 00:30 🍲	

American	Ingredients	Metric/Imperial
3	Shallots	3
2	Carrots	2
1	Onion	1
1	Leek, white part only	1
7 tbsp	Butter	90 g / 3½ oz
2 cups	Beef stock	500 ml / ¾ pint
1	Bouquet garni	1
	Cayenne pepper	
¼ lb	Large mushrooms	125 g / 4 oz
½	Lemon	½
2 oz	Cooked tongue	50 g / 2 oz
2 oz	Cooked ham	50 g / 2 oz
¼ cup	Port wine	4 tbsp
1 - 2 tbsp	Truffle peelings	1 - 2 tbsp
	Salt and pepper	

1. Peel and chop the shallots, carrots and onions. Chop the leek. Melt 3 tablespoons [40 g / 1½ oz] butter in a saucepan and add the chopped vegetables, stock, bouquet garni and a pinch of cayenne pepper. Bring to a boil and leave to reduce for 15 minutes.

2. Meanwhile, dice the mushrooms. Place them in a bowl of water to which the juice of ½ lemon has been added to prevent them from discoloring. Cut the tongue and ham into small cubes. Place the drained mushrooms, tongue and ham in a heavy saucepan and add the port, 2 tablespoons [25 g / 1 oz] butter and the truffle peelings. Cook over a low heat until the port has reduced by half.

3. Strain the brown sauce into the saucepan containing the tongue, mushrooms and truffles and cook for 2-3 minutes, stirring well. Add salt and pepper to taste.

4. Swirl in the remainder of the butter.

Sauce soubise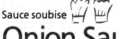

Onion Sauce

🔪 00:20   00:35 🍲

American	Ingredients	Metric/Imperial
10	Onions	10
1 cup	Stock or milk	250 ml / 8 fl oz
¼ cup	Butter	50 g / 2 oz
1 ¼ tbsp	Flour	1 ¼ tbsp
2 cups	Milk	500 ml / ¾ pint
	Grated nutmeg	
	Salt and pepper	

1. Peel and thinly slice the onions. Blanch them for 2 minutes in boiling water, then drain and rinse under cold running water. Drain again. Place them in a saucepan and cover with the stock or milk. Leave to cook gently for about 15 minutes.

2. Meanwhile, melt 2 tablespoons [25 g / 1 oz] butter in another saucepan. Add the flour and stir well. Cook gently, continuing to stir, for about 3 minutes. Add the milk, stirring vigorously. Bring to a boil and simmer for 10 minutes over a low heat.

3. When the onions have softened completely, increase the heat and boil off any liquid, stirring constantly. Purée the onions in a blender or food processor.

4. Add the onion purée to the sauce and heat, stirring.

5. Add a pinch of nutmeg, and salt and pepper to taste. Dot the remaining butter over the sauce to prevent a skin from forming and keep hot. Stir the sauce before serving.

Sauce Robert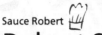

Robert Sauce

▭▭▷ 00:05		00:25 ⬭
American	**Ingredients**	**Metric/Imperial**
6	Onions	6
¼	Butter	50 g / 2 oz
3 tbsp	Flour	25 g / 1 oz
1 tbsp	Tomato paste [purée]	1 tbsp
⅔ cup	White wine	150 ml / ¼ pint
1 cup	Beef broth or stock	250 ml / 8 fl oz
	Salt and pepper	
2 tbsp	Prepared mustard	2 tbsp

1. Peel and thinly slice the onions. Heat the butter in a saucepan, add the onions and cook over a gentle heat, stirring frequently, until soft and golden. Add the flour and cook for a few minutes, continuing to stir.
2. Add the tomato paste. Stir in the white wine and broth. Add salt and pepper to taste. Leave to simmer for 20 minutes.
3. Add the mustard and mix thoroughly.

Sauce tomate

Tomato Sauce

▭▭▷ 00:10		00:45 ⬭
American	**Ingredients**	**Metric/Imperial**
3 lb	Tomatoes	1.5 kg / 3 lb
2	Small onions	2
2	Garlic cloves (optional)	2
⅔ cup	Olive oil	150 ml / ¼ pint
1	Bay leaf	1
1	Fresh thyme sprig	1
1	Bunch of fresh parsley	1
5	Fresh basil leaves or	5
1	Fresh tarragon sprig	1
	Salt and pepper	
1 - 2	Sugar cubes	1 - 2

1. Peel the tomatoes (first plunging them into boiling water for 10 seconds), remove the seeds and chop roughly. Peel and chop the onions and garlic.
2. Place the tomatoes, onions and garlic in a saucepan and add the oil, bay leaf, thyme, parsley and basil or tarragon. Add salt and pepper to taste. Cook over a high heat until excess liquid has completely evaporated. This will take about 40 minutes.
3. Taste and if you find the sauce too sharp, add the sugar cubes. Pass the sauce through a food mill or sieve.
4. You will obtain a more or less liquid sauce depending on the season and quality of the tomatoes. If after straining you find it rather thin, reduce it quickly over a brisk heat until it is of the desired consistency.
5. This sauce will keep for a week in the refrigerator.

SAUCES FOR COURSES

HORS D'OEUVRES

Avocats garnis

Stuffed Avocado

	00:30	00:00

American	Ingredients	Metric/Imperial
3	Avocados	3
	Lemon juice	
	Salt and pepper	
1	Celery stalk	1
6	Lettuce leaves	6
1 cup	Black olives	150 g / 5 oz

1. Cut the avocados in half lengthwise and remove the seed. Brush the cut surfaces with lemon juice to prevent them from discoloring. Season the avocados with salt and pepper to taste.
2. Trim and dice the celery. Place each avocado half on a lettuce leaf, surrounded by a few olives and a little diced celery. Fill the hollows in the avocado halves with one of the following preparations:

Anchovy vinaigrette: prepare a vinaigrette dressing and season to taste with anchovy paste or essence. Garnish the avocado with a few rolled anchovy fillets.

Shrimp: allow 1 tablespoon cooked peeled shrimps [prawns], a little diced celery and 1 tablespoon mayonnaise for each avocado half. Season with a few drops of tabasco sauce.

Crab: as for shrimp, using canned or freshly cooked crab meat and decorate with a few black olives.

Tuna: allow 1 tablespoon flaked canned tuna and a little diced celery dressed with vinaigrette or mayonnaise for each half avocado.

Artichauts vinaigrette

Artichokes Vinaigrette

	00:10	00:25 to 00:30

American	Ingredients	Metric/Imperial
6	Globe artichokes	6
	Salt and pepper	
1 tbsp	Vinegar	1 tbsp
1 tbsp	Prepared mustard, preferably Dijon	1 tbsp
3 tbsp	Oil	3 tbsp
1	Fresh parsley sprig	1

1. Break off the stalks of the artichokes, pulling them to remove the strings also. Remove any damaged or discolored leaves.

2. Bring a large saucepan of salted water to a boil. Add the artichokes and leave to cook for about 30 minutes. To test if they are done, pull out one of the large leaves near the base. If it comes out easily, the artichokes are ready.

3. Remove the artichokes from the water, and drain upside-down in a colander.

4. For the dressing, dissolve a pinch of salt in the vinegar. Stir in the mustard. Season with pepper to taste. Add the oil and chopped parsley and mix thoroughly.

5. Serve the vinaigrette with the warm or cold artichokes.

Asperges sauce mousseline

Asparagus with Mousseline Sauce

	00:20		00:35	

American	Ingredients	Metric/Imperial
3 lb	Asparagus	1.5 kg / 3 lb
⅔ cup	Vinegar	150 ml / ¼ pint
6	Black peppercorns	6
	Salt	
2	Egg yolks	2
6 tbsp	Butter	75 g / 3 oz
⅔ cup	Heavy [double] cream	150 ml / ¼ pint

1. Trim the woody ends from the asparagus, then scrape the stalks. Tie the asparagus spears in 4 equal bunches, and set aside.

2. Place the vinegar and peppercorns in a small saucepan and bring to a boil. Boil until reduced to 1 tablespoon.

3. Meanwhile, put salted water on to boil in a large saucepan. When the water is boiling, add the bunches of asparagus. As soon as boiling resumes, reduce the heat to keep the water simmering. Leave to cook for 5-20 minutes (depending on the age and size of the asparagus) or until tender.

4. When the asparagus is cooked, remove it from the water and drain well. Arrange on a folded napkin on a warmed serving dish and keep hot.

5. Strain the peppercorns from the reduced vinegar. Remove the pan from the heat and add the egg yolks, whisking vigorously. Gradually incorporate the butter, cut into small pieces, continuing to whisk until thickened. Add salt to taste.

6. Whip the cream until thick and fold into the sauce.

7. Serve the mousseline sauce in a sauceboat with the asparagus.

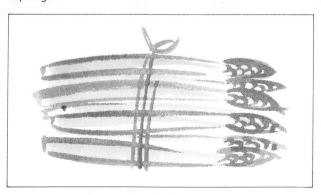

Aspics de foies de volaille

Chicken Livers in Aspic

	00:20 plus chilling		00:08	

American	Ingredients	Metric/Imperial
1	Shallot	1
3 tbsp	Butter	40 g / 1 ½ oz
1 lb	Chicken livers	500 g / 1 lb
	Salt and pepper	
	Dried thyme	
1 tbsp	Cognac	1 tbsp
1 quart	Liquid aspic (see page 17)	1 l / 1 ¾ pints
	Lettuce or other salad greens	
2 - 3	Tomatoes	2 - 3

1. Peel the shallot and chop finely. Melt the butter in a saucepan over a moderate heat, add the shallot and cook until softened.
2. Halve the livers and add to the pan. Cook over a brisk heat until they are firm and browned but still pink inside.
3. Add salt and pepper to taste. Add a pinch of thyme and the cognac. Remove from the heat and allow to cool completely.
4. Divide the livers between six individual molds and cover with warm aspic. Chill for at least 6 hours or until set.
5. Unmold the livers in aspic onto serving dishes garnished with salad greens and tomato quarters.

Fonds d'artichaut farcis

Stuffed Artichoke Hearts

	00:30		01:00	

American	Ingredients	Metric/Imperial
6	Large globe artichokes	6
	Lemon juice	
	Salt and pepper	
½ lb	Cooked ham	250 g / 8 oz
½ lb	Button mushrooms	250 g / 8 oz
5 tbsp	Butter	65 g / 2 ½ oz
2 tbsp	Flour	2 tbsp
1 ⅓ cups	Milk	325 ml / 11 fl oz
	Grated nutmeg	
1 cup	Grated gruyère cheese	125 g / 4 oz
2 tbsp	Crème fraîche	2 tbsp

1. Remove the leaves and hairy choke from the artichokes. Peel the hearts with a knife, rubbing with lemon juice as you go along, so that they do not discolour. Cook the artichoke hearts in boiling salted water for 30-40 minutes or until the point of a knife will go through them easily.
2. Meanwhile, chop the ham. Chop the mushrooms and moisten with a few drops of lemon juice to keep them white. Heat 2 tablespoons [25 g / 1 oz] of the butter in a saucepan, add the mushrooms and cook until all the moisture has evaporated. Remove from the heat and mix the mushrooms with the chopped ham.

3. Preheat the oven to 400°F / 200°C / Gas Mark 6.

4. Melt the remaining butter in another saucepan over a gentle heat and add the flour. Stir well, then gradually stir in the milk and a pinch of grated nutmeg. Season to taste with salt and pepper, and leave to simmer for 10 minutes over a low heat, stirring occasionally.

5. Add 4 tablespoons of the white sauce and about one-third of the gruyère cheese to the ham and mushroom mixture, and mix well. Fill the drained artichoke hearts with the mixture, and arrange in an ovenproof dish.

6. Add the crème fraîche and remaining cheese to the rest of the white sauce. Mix and pour over the artichoke hearts.

7. Place in the oven and bake for 15-20 minutes.

Endives au jambon

Endives [Chicory] with Ham

	00:10		01:10	

American	Ingredients	Metric/Imperial
12	Medium-sized heads of endive [chicory]	12
½ cup	Butter	125 g / 4 oz
2 tsp	Sugar	2 tsp
	Salt and pepper	
1 tbsp	Flour	2 tbsp
⅔ cup	Milk	150 ml / ¼ pint
1 cup	Crème fraîche	250 ml / 8 fl oz
½ cup	Grated gruyère cheese	50 g / 2 oz
	Grated nutmeg	
12	Thin slices of cooked ham	12
12	Thin slices of gruyère cheese	12

1. Remove the damaged leaves from the endives [chicory]. Using a pointed knife, remove the hard part from the base of the leaves by hollowing out the center. Wash and drain.

2. Melt 2 tablespoons [25 g / 1 oz] butter in a thick-bottomed saucepan. When it froths, add the endives, sugar and salt and pepper to taste. Leave to cook over a gentle heat for approximately 40 minutes. The endives are done when they are slightly browned and the point of a knife can pass through them easily.

3. Meanwhile, melt 1 tablespoon butter in another thick-bottomed saucepan. Add the flour and cook, stirring, for 1 minute. Remove the saucepan from the heat and gradually add the milk, continuing to stir. Return to the heat and cook, stirring, until thickened. Add the crème fraîche, half of the grated gruyère, a pinch of nutmeg, and salt and pepper to taste. Leave to cook for 5 minutes over a gentle heat, stirring continuously.

4. Preheat the oven to 425°F / 220°C / Gas Mark 7.

5. On each slice of ham, place a slice of gruyère and then a braised endive. Roll up the ham which should go right around the endive. Arrange the rolls in a buttered ovenproof dish. Cover them with the sauce and sprinkle with the remaining grated gruyère.

6. Bake for about 30 minutes. Serve in the cooking dish.

Escargots de Bourgogne

Snails with Garlic Butter

	01:00		00:30	
	plus standing time			

American	Ingredients	Metric/Imperial
2 oz	Shallots	50 g / 2 oz
2	Garlic cloves	2
1 lb (2 cups)	Butter, at room temperature	500 g / 1 lb
2 tbsp	Chopped fresh parsley	2 tbsp
	Salt and pepper	
72	Canned snails with shells	72

1. Prepare the snail butter: peel and finely chop the shallots and garlic. Mix with the butter. Add the parsley and mash the mixture with a fork to blend thoroughly. Season to taste with salt and pepper.

2. Drain the snails. Drop them into a pan of simmering water and cook for 5 minutes. Drain, cool with cold water and drain again.

3. Put a pat of snail butter in each snail shell. Put the snails in the shells and fill with the rest of the snail butter.

4. Leave the snails in a cool place for 24 hours so that they absorb the flavor of the garlic butter.

5. Preheat the oven to 325°F / 160°C / Gas Mark 3.

6. Arrange the snails on snail dishes and put in the oven. Bake until the butter has melted and the snails are piping hot.

SHELLFISH

Écrevisses cardinalisées

Crayfish in Piquant Wine Sauce

	00:15		01:40	

American	Ingredients	Metric/Imperial
1	Carrot	1
2	Onions	2
5	Shallots	5
2	Garlic cloves	2
1 oz	Fresh pork back fat	25 g / 1 oz
⅔ cup	Dry white wine	150 ml / ¼ pint
⅔ cup	White wine vinegar	150 ml / ¼ pint
⅓ cup	Meat gravy	5 tbsp
2½ tbsp	Brandy	2½ tbsp
2	Fresh thyme sprigs	2
½	Bay leaf	½
	Grated rind of ¼ orange	
1 tbsp	Sea salt	1 tbsp
1 tbsp	Black peppercorns	1 tbsp
	Ground white pepper	
	Cayenne pepper	
36	Crayfish	36

1. Peel the carrot, onions, shallots and garlic and chop them into dice. Cut the pork fat into small dice. Put the diced vegetables and pork fat into a stewpan and add the wine, wine vinegar, gravy, brandy, thyme sprigs, bay leaf, orange rind, sea salt, peppercorns, 2 pinches of ground white pepper and a pinch of cayenne pepper.
2. Bring to a boil and cook very gently until the sauce has reduced by half (about 1½ hours).
3. Meanwhile, rinse the crayfish and clean them by pulling out the central fin of the tail, to remove the small black vein or bowel. Pat dry with paper towels.
4. When the sauce has reduced, put in the crayfish and leave to cook for about 10 minutes.
5. Remove the crayfish with a slotted spoon and pile up in a serving dish. Strain the sauce and serve with the crayfish.

Mouclade

Mussels in Wine and Cream

🔪 00:10		🍲 00:20

American	Ingredients	Metric/Imperial
3 quarts	Fresh mussels	2 kg / 4 lb
2	Onions	2
1	Fresh thyme sprig	1
1	Bay leaf	1
1 ¼ cups	Dry white wine	300 ml / ½ pint
½	Lemon	½
	Curry powder	
	Salt and pepper	
2 tbsp	Crème fraîche	2 tbsp

1. Scrub the mussels thoroughly and rinse in cold water. Peel and chop the onions.
2. Place the mussels in a large pan with the onions, thyme sprig, bay leaf and wine. Cover and cook until all the mussels open. (Discard any that remain closed.)
3. Take the mussels out of the pan, discarding the empty half-shells. Keep the mussels on the half-shell hot in a dish.
4. Heat up the cooking juices and add the juice of the ½ lemon, a pinch of curry powder and salt and pepper to taste. At the last minute, stir in the crème fraîche. Pour the sauce over the mussels and serve immediately.

Coquilles Saint-Jacques au beurre blanc

Scallops with White Butter Sauce

🔪 00:30		🍲 00:30

American	Ingredients	Metric/Imperial
18	Sea scallops	18
	Court-bouillon	
10	Shallots	10
⅔ cup	Cider vinegar	150 ml / ¼ pint
1 cup	Very cold butter	250 g / 8 oz
	Pepper	

1. Cut each scallop into 2-3 slices. Put them in a saucepan with their coral, if available, and just cover with court-bouillon. Bring slowly to a boil over a medium heat, then allow to simmer for 4-5 minutes.
2. Meanwhile, prepare the white butter sauce. Peel the shallots and chop them finely. Put them in a saucepan with the cider vinegar. Cook over a low heat until the shallots are soft and all the vinegar has evaporated. Cut the butter into small pieces and add little by little to the shallots, whisking vigorously. The mixture must not be allowed to boil. Season to taste with pepper.

3. Drain the scallops, arrange them on a serving dish and cover with the sauce. Serve immediately.

Cook's tip: if you prefer a smoother sauce, put it through a strainer before adding it to the scallops.

Homards à l'américaine

Lobsters in Rich Tomato Sauce

American	Ingredients	Metric/Imperial
	00:40	00:25
2	Carrots	2
3	Onions	3
2	Shallots	2
1	Garlic clove	1
3	Tomatoes	3
1 cup	Butter	250 g / 8 oz
1 tbsp	Oil	1 tbsp
3 (1 ½ lb)	Live lobsters	3 (750 g / 1 ½ lb)
⅓ cup	Brandy	5 tbsp
1 tbsp	Tomato paste [purée]	1 tbsp
2 cups	Dry white wine	500 ml / ¾ pint
1	Bouquet garni	1
	Cayenne pepper	
	Salt and pepper	
1 tbsp	Chopped fresh parsley	1 tbsp

1. Peel the carrots and grate them. Peel and chop the onions and shallots. Peel and crush the garlic. Peel the tomatoes (first plunging them in boiling water for 10 seconds) and chop the flesh roughly.
2. Heat 1 tablespoon of butter and the oil in a large saucepan. Add the carrots, onions and shallots. Cook over a low heat until all the ingredients have softened.
3. Meanwhile, cut up the lobsters. First sever the spinal cord by plunging a knife into the crack on top of the back between the body and tail sections. This will kill the lobster. Cut off the claws and cut the tail section from the body. Cut the tail into sections. Remove the greenish liver, or tomalley, and coral if any and put them in a mixing bowl.
4. Add the claws and tail sections to the saucepan and stir well until the shell turns red. Add the brandy and set it alight. Shake the pan gently until the flame goes out.
5. Mix the tomato paste with the wine and tomatoes. Add to the pan with the bouquet garni, garlic, a pinch of cayenne pepper, and salt and pepper to taste. Cover and cook over a medium heat for 20 minutes.
6. Remove the lobster pieces with a slotted spoon and put them on a dish. Add 2 tablespoons [25 g / 1 oz] of the butter to the lobster liver and mix well. Add this mixture to the sauce with the chopped parsley. Boil for 3 minutes over a high heat, stirring, then taste and adjust the seasoning.
7. Take the saucepan off the heat and add the rest of the butter, cut into small pieces. Whisk vigorously until the sauce is well bound. Discard the bouquet garni. Put the lobster pieces back into the sauce, reheat gently and serve immediately.

Huîtres chaudes au champagne

Hot Oysters with Champagne

	00:30	00:30
American	**Ingredients**	**Metric/Imperial**
36	Oysters	36
2	Shallots	2
1 tbsp	Butter	1 tbsp
¼ cup	Crème fraîche	4 tbsp
⅔ cup	Champagne	150 ml / ¼ pint
1 quantity	Hollandaise sauce	1 quantity

1. Open the oysters, reserving the liquor, and set them aside on the half shell. Pour the liquor into a saucepan.
2. Peel and chop the shallots. Add them to the saucepan with the butter. Cook gently until the shallots become translucent. Add 2 tablespoons of the crème fraîche and the champagne. Leave to reduce over a low heat, stirring occasionally.
3. Meanwhile, whip the remaining crème until stiff.
4. Preheat the oven to 500°F / 250°C / Gas Mark 9.
5. Add the reduced champagne mixture to the hollandaise sauce, whisking vigorously. Fold in the whipped crème.
6. Coat each oyster with the sauce and put them on a baking sheet in the oven. Bake for a few minutes to brown. Serve hot.

Coquilles Saint-Jacques Newburg

Scallops Newburg

	00:10	00:20 to 00:25
American	**Ingredients**	**Metric/Imperial**
24	Sea scallops	24
	Flour	
2 tbsp	Butter	25 g / 1 oz
2 tbsp	Brandy	2 tbsp
¾ cup	Madeira wine	175 ml / 6 fl oz
	Salt and pepper	
1	Small can of truffle peelings	1
1 cup	Crème fraîche	250 ml / 8 fl oz
3	Egg yolks	3

1. Cut each scallop into 2 or 3 slices; coat lightly in flour.
2. Melt the butter in a frying pan, add the scallops and cook until they are firm but not browned (about 2 minutes on each side). Add the brandy, madeira, and salt and pepper to taste. Boil briskly until the sauce is thick enough to coat the scallops.
3. Reserve some of the truffle for the garnish. Add the rest to the frying pan with the liquid in the can and 3 tablespoons of the crème fraîche. Cook over a low heat for 5-8 minutes, stirring from time to time.
4. Mix the egg yolks with the rest of the crème. Add this mixture to the pan and stir to thicken over a medium heat. Do not allow to boil.
5. Serve sprinkled with the reserved truffle.

FISH

Lotte à l'américaine

Monkfish in Tomato Sauce

00:15   00:25

American	Ingredients	Metric/Imperial
½ lb	Onions	250 g / 8 oz
2	Shallots	2
2	Garlic cloves	2
5	Tomatoes	5
3 lb	Monkfish fillet	1.5 kg / 3 lb
	Flour	
¼ cup	Olive oil	4 tbsp
2 tbsp	Brandy	2 tbsp
½	Bottle of dry white wine	½
1	Bouquet garni	1
2	Sugar cubes	2
1 tbsp	Tomato paste [purée]	1 tbsp
	Salt and pepper	
	Cayenne pepper	

1. Peel and chop the onions, shallots and garlic. Peel the tomatoes (first plunging them in boiling water for 10 seconds), remove the seeds and coarsely chop the flesh. Cut the fish into pieces and coat them in flour.
2. Heat 1 tablespoon of oil in a saucepan, add the onions, shallots and garlic and soften over a low heat, stirring frequently.
3. Heat the rest of the oil in a frying pan, add the pieces of fish and cook until the fish is golden brown on all sides.
4. Add the brandy to the fish and set it alight. When the flames die down, add the fish and its juices to the vegetables in the saucepan. Add the wine, bouquet garni, tomatoes, sugar and tomato paste. Season to taste with salt, pepper and cayenne.
5. Bring to a boil, then cover and cook over a low heat for 20-25 minutes. Serve hot.

Filets de sole normande

Normandy Style Sole

| | 00:20 | | 00:40 | |

American	Ingredients	Metric/Imperial
4 (¾ lb)	Soles, filleted (bones reserved)	4 (350 g / 12 oz)
	Court-bouillon	
	Hard [dry] cider	
⅔ cup	Water	150 ml / ¼ pint
1 pint	Fresh mussels	500 g / 1 lb
1 tbsp	Butter	1 tbsp
1 tbsp	Flour	1 tbsp
¼ cup	Crème fraîche	4 tbsp
	Grated nutmeg	
	Salt and pepper	

1. Roll up each sole fillet and secure with a wooden toothpick. Arrange all the fish rolls in a frying pan or flameproof casserole. Pour over half court-bouillon and half cider, enough liquid to cover the fish. Heat until the liquid simmers. Turn the fish rolls and cook for a further 5 minutes.
2. Remove the fish rolls with a slotted spatula and keep hot.
3. Add the fish bones to the pan with the water and simmer gently for 15 minutes.
4. Meanwhile, scrub the mussels thoroughly. Put them in a saucepan, cover and heat briskly, shaking the pan, until they open (discard any that remain closed). Remove the mussels from their shells, reserving all the liquid from the shells, and keep hot. Strain the liquid. Also strain the cider mixture.
5. Heat the butter in a saucepan, add the flour and stir for 2 minutes. Add crème fraîche and bring to a boil, stirring. Gradually blend in the strained mussel liquid and cider to obtain a thick cream sauce. Add a pinch of nutmeg and season to taste with salt and pepper. Stir in the mussels.

Haddock charentaise

Smoked Haddock with Cream Sauce

| | 00:10 | | 00:20 | |

American	Ingredients	Metric/Imperial
3-4	Small smoked haddock	3-4
2 cups	Milk	500 ml / ¾ pint
5 tbsp	Butter	65 g / 2½ oz
1 cup	Crème fraîche	250 ml / 8 fl oz
	Salt and pepper	
	Grated nutmeg	
	Lemon juice	

1. Put the fish in a saucepan, add the milk and enough water just to cover the fish and bring to a boil over a medium heat.

Remove from the heat and leave to poach, covered, for 10-15 minutes. Drain and keep warm.

2. Meanwhile, put 6 tablespoons of the fish cooking liquid in a small bowl or saucepan and add the butter, cut into small pieces, and crème fraîche. Put the bowl or saucepan over another saucepan containing water and heat, whisking, until the mixture will coat the back of a spoon. Season to taste with salt, pepper and nutmeg and a few drops of lemon juice.

3. Arrange the fish on a serving dish and serve with the sauce.

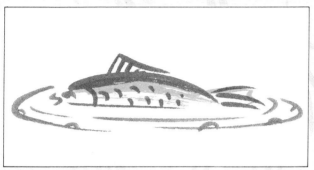

Saumon froid

Cold Poached Salmon with Piquant Mayonnaise

	00:30	01:00
	Serves 15–20	

American	Ingredients	Metric/Imperial
1 (6 lb)	Salmon, cleaned	1 (3 kg / 6 lb)
1	Bottle of dry white wine	1
1	Court-bouillon	
3 cups	Mayonnaise	750 ml / 1¼ pints
1 tsp	Tabasco sauce	1 tsp
3 tbsp	Chopped fresh parsley	3 tbsp
2 tbsp	Chopped fresh tarragon	2 tbsp
3 tbsp	Chopped fresh chervil	3 tbsp
2	Gherkins	2
1 tbsp	Capers	1 tbsp
1	Garlic clove	1
1	Shallot	1
	Salt and pepper	

1. Put the salmon in a fish kettle. Pour in the wine and add enough court-bouillon to cover the fish completely. Heat rapidly until the liquid simmers, then continue simmering for 1 hour.

2. Take the fish kettle off the heat and leave the salmon to cool in the liquid. Keep in a cool place for 12 hours.

3. Drain the salmon and skin it carefully. Place it on a serving dish. Strain the cooking liquid and chill until it begins to set.

4. Meanwhile, combine the mayonnaise, tabasco sauce, parsley, tarragon and chervil. Finely chop the gherkins and capers. Peel and finely chop the garlic and shallot. Add to the mayonnaise. Taste and adjust the seasoning. Chill.

5. Paint several layers of the setting fish cooking liquid on the salmon with a pastry brush. Chill until set. Serve with the mayonnaise.

POULTRY & GAME

Poulet à l'estragon

Chicken with Tarragon

	00:15		00:55	

American	Ingredients	Metric/Imperial
1 (4 lb)	Chicken	1 (1.8 kg / 4 lb)
3 tbsp	Oil	3 tbsp
¼ cup	Butter	50 g / 2 oz
6	Shallots	6
1	Carrot	1
2 tbsp	Brandy	2 tbsp
1 cup	White wine	250 ml / 8 fl oz
	Salt and pepper	
4	Fresh tarragon sprigs	4
1 cup	Crème fraîche	250 ml / 8 fl oz
1	Egg yolk	1
1 tsp	Flour	1 tsp
1	Fresh chervil sprig	1

1. Cut the chicken into pieces.
2. Heat the oil and 3 tablespoons [40 g / 1½ oz] butter in a flameproof casserole. Add the pieces of chicken and cook over a low heat for about 20 minutes, until lightly browned. Turn frequently and do not allow the butter to burn.
3. Meanwhile, peel and thinly slice the shallots and carrot.
4. Remove the chicken from the casserole and keep hot.
5. Add the remaining butter to the casserole, then put in the shallots and carrot. Cook for 5 minutes, then put in the chicken. Sprinkle with the brandy and set alight.
6. When the flames have died out, add the white wine and a little water so that the liquid covers the pieces of chicken. Season to taste with salt and pepper and add 2 of the tarragon sprigs. Cover the casserole, bring to a boil and simmer over a low heat for 30 minutes.
7. Remove the pieces of chicken from the casserole and arrange them on a serving platter. Keep hot.
8. Beat the crème fraîche in a mixing bowl with the egg yolk and flour, pour this into the cooking juices and heat, stirring well. When the sauce has thickened, pour it over the chicken through a strainer.
9. Finely chop the rest of the tarragon and the chervil and sprinkle over the chicken.

Aspic de volaille

Chicken in Aspic

American	Ingredients	Metric/Imperial
3 quarts	Water	3 l / 5 pints
3	Carrots	3
3	Leeks	3
3	Onions	3
2	Cloves	2
2	Celery stalks	2
	Salt and pepper	
1	Bouquet garni	1
1 (3 lb)	Chicken	1 (1.5 kg / 3 lb)
2 envelopes	Unflavored gelatin	2 sachets
1 (½ lb)	Slice of cooked ham	1 (250 g / 8 oz)
1	Truffle (optional)	1
½ lb	Pâté de foie gras	250 g / 8 oz

1. Bring the water to a boil in a large pan. Meanwhile, peel the carrots. Cut the leeks into quarters. Peel the onions and stud one with 2 cloves. Add the carrots, leeks, onions and celery to the boiling water. Season with salt and pepper, add the bouquet garni and simmer gently for 30 minutes.

2. Add the chicken and cook for 1 hour.

3. Remove the chicken and set aside. Strain the cooking liquid through a strainer into a bowl, then through a fine strainer into a saucepan. Bring to a boil and simmmer until the liquid is reduced to 1 quart [1 l / 1¾ pints].

4. Dissolve the gelatin following the instructions on the package. Stir into the reduced cooking liquid and allow to cool until syrupy.

5. Pour a ½ in / 1 cm layer of the cooking liquid onto the bottom of an oiled 1½ quart [1.5 l / 2½ pint] charlotte mold. Chill until set.

6. Meanwhile, cut a ½ in / 1 cm wide strip from the slice of ham and dice it. Remove the chicken meat from the carcass, discarding all skin, and thinly slice the meat. Slice the truffle.

7. Arrange the truffle slices, diced ham and a few slices of chicken on the set aspic at the bottom of the mold. Cover with another layer of still liquid aspic and leave to set in the refrigerator.

8. Cut the rest of the ham into thin strips. Fold into the pâté. Remove the mold from the refrigerator and add a layer of the ham-pâté mixture. Cover with slices of chicken, then alternate the chicken and ham-pâté mixture until all the ingredients are used up.

9. Pour most of the remaining cold, but still liquid, aspic into the mold (warm the aspic again before pouring, if necessary), making sure that the aspic fills all the gaps between the mold and the filling.

10. Cover with a board, place a weight on top and chill for 6 hours.

11. To remove the chicken in aspic from the mold, carefully slide the blade of a knife between the aspic and the edge of the mold or plunge the mold into hot water for a few moments only. Place an inverted serving dish on top of the mold and turn them both over, in one swift movement, to turn out the chicken in aspic. Cut the rest of the aspic into small dice and arrange it around the chicken in aspic. Serve well chilled.

Lièvre à la crème

Hare with Cream Sauce

00:15   01:30 to 02:00

American	Ingredients	Metric/Imperial
¼ cup	Butter	50 g / 2 oz
1 (4 lb)	Young hare	1 (2 kg / 4 lb)
4	Shallots	4
1 (½ lb)	Slice of cooked ham	1 (250 g / 8 oz)
⅓ cup	Vinegar	5 tbsp
⅔ cup	Dry white wine	150 ml / ¼ pint
	Salt and pepper	
1 cup	Crème fraîche	250 ml / 8 fl oz
1 tbsp	Cornstarch [cornflour]	1 tbsp

1. Melt the butter in a flameproof casserole, add the hare and brown on all sides.
2. Peel and finely chop the shallots. Add them to the casserole with the slice of ham. Cook for 2-3 minutes, then pour in the vinegar and one-third of the wine. Season to taste.
3. Cover and cook over a very low heat for 1 hour, adding the rest of the wine during this time.
4. Add the crème fraîche and cook for a further 30 minutes to 1 hour or until the hare is very tender.
5. Remove the ham, shallots and hare to a deep serving dish. Mix the cornstarch with 2 tablespoons of the cooking liquid and add to the casserole. Cook over a low heat until the sauce thickens. Pour over the hare and serve immediately.

Poulet à la crème

Chicken with Cream and Mushroom Sauce

00:25   00:45

American	Ingredients	Metric/Imperial
1 (3 lb)	Chicken	1 (1.5 kg / 3 lb)
	Salt and pepper	
3 tbsp + 1 tsp	Butter	40g / 1½ oz + 1 tsp
3 tbsp	Oil	3 tbsp
1	Thin bacon slice	1
1 lb	Button mushrooms	500 g / 1 lb
½	Lemon	½
4	Shallots	4
1¼ cups	White wine	300 ml / ½ pint
1 tsp	Flour	1 tsp
1¼ cups	Crème fraîche	300 ml / ½ pint

1. Cut the chicken into 6 pieces and season with salt and pepper. Heat 3 tablespoons [40 g / 1½ oz] butter with 2 tablespoons of the oil in a flameproof casserole. Add the pieces of chicken and brown on all sides over a medium heat.
2. Meanwhile, cut the bacon into small strips. Dice the

mushrooms and sprinkle them with the juice of the ½ lemon. Peel and chop the shallots. Gently fry the strips of bacon in a frying pan without any fat, then drain them and set aside.

3. Heat the remaining oil in the frying pan. Add the mushrooms and shallots and cook until all the liquid has evaporated. Season to taste with salt and pepper.

4. Add the bacon, mushrooms and shallots to the casserole. Pour in the white wine. Cover and cook over a medium heat for 40 minutes.

5. Blend the flour with a teaspoon of butter to a paste.

6. Drain the pieces of chicken and put them on a warm serving platter. Add the crème fraîche to the casserole, then add the butter and flour paste and thicken over a brisk heat, stirring. Adjust the seasoning.

7. Pour this sauce over the chicken and serve immediately.

Faisans bohémienne

Bohemian Style Pheasant

	00:30	00:40	
	plus standing time		

American	Ingredients	Metric/Imperial
½ lb	Fresh foie gras	250 g / 8 oz
	Paprika	
½ cup	Butter	125 g / 4 oz
	Salt and pepper	
2	Young pheasants	2
6	Slices of bread ½ in / 1 cm thick	6
¼ cup	Brandy	4 tbsp
½ cup	Crème fraîche	125 ml / 4 fl oz

1. Cut the foie gras into dice and roll it lightly in paprika. Leave for 1 hour to absorb the flavor.

2. Preheat the oven to 425°F / 220°C / Gas Mark 7.

3. Melt 1 teaspoon of butter in a frying pan, add the diced foie gras and brown lightly. Season with salt, then remove from the pan with a slotted spoon and allow to cool. Put aside the frying pan containing the butter.

4. Stuff the pheasants with the foie gras and sew up the openings with kitchen string. Put the pheasants in a roasting pan and roast for 40 minutes, turning them over carefully after 20 minutes.

5. Just before the pheasants have finished cooking, cut the crusts from the bread and cut each slice in half, diagonally. Heat the rest of the butter in the frying pan used earlier and fry the slices of bread until golden brown on both sides.

6. Heat the brandy in a saucepan. Pour it over the pheasants and set alight. When the flames have died away, remove the string from the pheasants and catch the juices which run out in the pan. Add the crème fraîche and a pinch of paprika to the juices. Heat, stirring to loosen all the sediment at the bottom.

7. Spread the pieces of fried bread with the melted foie gras. Put the pheasants on a serving platter, pour the sauce over them and surround with the garnished fried bread. Serve.

Poulet Vallée d'Auge

Auge Valley Chicken

	00:15	01:15

American	Ingredients	Metric/Imperial
1 (4 lb)	Chicken	1 (2 kg / 4 lb)
⅔ cup	Butter	150 g / 5 oz
	Salt and pepper	
¼ cup	Calvados or applejack	4 tbsp
1 ¼ cups	Thick crème fraîche	300 ml / ½ pint

1. Cut the chicken into pieces.
2. Heat the butter in a flameproof casserole, add the chicken and brown for about 10 minutes. Season with salt and pepper. Cover and cook over a very low heat for 1 hour.
3. Pour the calvados into the casserole, heat and set alight. When the flames have died out, remove the pieces of chicken, arrange them on a warmed serving platter and keep hot.
4. Add the crème fraîche to the liquid, stir and bring to a boil. Simmer for 5-6 minutes or until the sauce has thickened. Pour the sauce over the chicken and serve immediately.

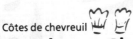

Côtes de chevreuil

Venison Chops with Game Sauce

	00:10	00:08

American	Ingredients	Metric/Imperial
2 tbsp	Red currant jelly	2 tbsp
2 tbsp	Crème fraîche	2 tbsp
1 cup	Game sauce	250 mll / 8 fl oz
6	Slices of bread	6
3 tbsp	Butter	40 g / 1 ½ oz
3 tbsp	Olive oil	3 tbsp
6	Venison chops	6
	Salt and pepper	

1. Add the red currant jelly and crème fraîche to the game sauce and stir to mix. Keep hot in a bowl or pan placed in a saucepan containing hot water.
2. Cut the crusts from the bread. Heat 1 tablespoon [15 g / ½ oz] butter and oil in a frying pan and fry the bread slices until golden brown on both sides. Remove from the pan and keep hot.
3. Heat the remaining butter and oil in the frying pan. Add the venison chops and cook for about 4 minutes on each side, or until well browned and cooked to your taste. Season with salt and pepper.
4. Put the chops on the fried bread and serve immediately with the sauce.

Poulet au whisky

Chicken with Whiskey Sauce

⬤ 00:15		🍲 00:50
American	**Ingredients**	**Metric/Imperial**
1 (4 lb)	Chicken	1 (1.8 kg / 4 lb)
6 tbsp	Butter	75 g / 3 oz
⅔ cup	Whiskey	150 ml / ¼ pint
5 oz	Button mushrooms	150 g / 5 oz
	Lemon juice	
1	Shallot	1
½ cup	Crème fraîche	125 ml / 4 fl oz
	Salt and pepper	
1 tsp	Cornstarch [cornflour]	1 tsp

1. Cut the chicken into quarters. Heat 2 tablespoons [25 g / 1 oz] butter in a flameproof casserole, add the chicken pieces and cook over a medium heat for about 10 minutes or until golden on all sides.

2. Pour the whiskey over the chicken. Remove from the heat, cover and leave to steep for 10 minutes.

3. Meanwhile, quarter the mushrooms and sprinkle with a few drops of lemon juice. Peel and chop the shallot. Melt the rest of the butter in a frying pan, add the mushrooms and cook, stirring occasionally, until all the liquid has evaporated. Add the chopped shallot and cook for a few minutes longer.

4. Put the mushrooms and shallot in the casserole with the chicken, add half the crème fraîche and season with salt and pepper. Cover and cook over a medium heat for about 30 minutes or until the chicken pieces are tender.

5. Arrange the pieces of chicken on a serving platter and keep hot. Return the casserole to the heat and bring back to a boil. Mix together the remaining crème fraîche and cornstarch and add to the sauce, whisking well. Cook, stirring, until thickened. Add a few drops of lemon juice. Adjust the seasoning and pour the sauce over the pieces of chicken.

MEAT DISHES
Beef

Estouffade de boeuf

Beef in Red Wine Sauce

00:20   03:30 to 04:00

American	Ingredients	Metric/Imperial
1 lb	Chuck steak	500 g / 1 lb
1 ½ lb	Flank steak	750 g / 1 ½ lb
½ lb	Lightly salted bacon	250 g / 8 oz
4	Onions	4
2	Garlic cloves	2
2 tbsp	Olive oil	2 tbsp
¼ cup	Flour	25 g / 1 oz
	Salt and pepper	
1	Bottle of red wine	1
1	Bouquet garni	1
½ lb	Button mushrooms	250 g / 8 oz
1 tbsp	Tomato paste [purée]	1 tbsp
⅔ cup	Black olives	125 g / 4 oz

1. Cut the meat into chunks. Cut the bacon into strips. Blanch the bacon in a pan of boiling water for 5 minutes, then drain and pat dry with paper towels. Peel and quarter the onions. Peel and crush the garlic.

2. Preheat the oven to 350°F / 180°C / Gas Mark 4.

3. Heat 1 tablespoon of oil in a flameproof casserole over a medium heat, add the bacon and cook until golden brown. Remove with a slotted spoon.

4. Coat the meat in the flour. Add to the casserole and brown on all sides. Season with salt and pepper and pour over the wine. Bring to a boil over a high heat and reduce the liquid to about half.

5. Add just enough water to cover the meat. Add the garlic and bouquet garni, then cover the casserole with a sheet of foil and put the lid on top. Transfer to the oven and cook for 3 hours.

6. Meanwhile, quarter the mushrooms. Heat the rest of the oil in a frying pan, add the mushrooms and cook until all their liquid has evaporated. Set aside.

7. Pour the meat mixture into a strainer placed over a large bowl. Return the meat to the casserole together with the bacon and mushrooms.

8. Skim the fat from the cooking liquid. Add the tomato paste and olives. Adjust the seasoning if necessary by adding a little salt and pepper, then pour the sauce over the meat in the casserole. Cover and cook over a gentle heat for 20-25 minutes longer. Serve with rice or noodles.

Chateaubriands au poivre et au madère

Pepper Steak in Madeira Sauce

	00:10	00:04 to 00:08	

American	Ingredients	Metric/Imperial
3 tbsp	Crushed black peppercorns	3 tbsp
6 (½ lb)	Boneless sirloin [fillet] steak	6 (250 g / 8 oz)
⅔ cup	Butter	150 g / 5 oz
	Salt	
¼ cup	Brandy	4 tbsp
1 tsp	Potato starch or flour or cornstarch [cornflour]	1 tsp
1 cup	Madeira wine	250 ml / 8 fl oz

1. Sprinkle a chopping board or worktop with the crushed peppercorns and press both sides of each steak into them. Press with the palm of the hand to ensure the peppercorns stick to the meat well.

2. Heat ¼ cup [50 g / 2 oz] of the butter in a large frying pan. When it has turned golden brown, reduce the heat and add the steaks. Cook for 2-4 minutes on each side according to individual taste. Sprinkle with a little salt.

3. Pour the brandy over the steaks and set alight, lifting the steaks up so that the flames burn all over them. Remove the steaks with a slotted spoon, arrange on a serving dish and keep hot.

4. Dissolve the potato starch or cornstarch in 1 tablespoon of the madeira. Pour the rest of the madeira into the frying pan and bring to a boil, scraping the bottom of the pan with a wooden spatula. Remove the pan from the heat and add the dissolved potato starch. Return to a medium heat and stir until the sauce is slightly thickened. Remove from the heat again and gradually add the rest of the butter, cut into small pieces, whisking constantly.

5. Pour the sauce over the steaks and serve.

Émincé de boeuf

Beef Strips in Mustard Sauce

🔪 00:15		00:20 🥘
American	**Ingredients**	**Metric/Imperial**
2 lb	Boneless sirloin [rump] steak	1 kg / 2 lb
4	Shallots	4
¼ cup	Butter	50 g / 2 oz
1 cup	Crème fraîche	250 ml / 8 fl oz
1 tsp	Strong prepared mustard	1 tsp
	Salt and pepper	

1. Trim any fat from the steak, then cut into slices ¼ in / 5 mm thick. Cut these slices into strips ¼ in / 5 mm wide. Peel and finely chop the shallots.
2. Heat half of the butter in a frying pan and add half of the meat strips. Cook over high heat, stirring, until browned all over. Remove with a slotted spoon. Brown the rest of the meat strips and remove.
3. Melt the rest of the butter in the frying pan over a medium heat, add the shallots and cook until soft and translucent. Add 4 tablespoons of the crème fraîche and stir, scraping the bottom of the pan with a wooden spatula. Cook until the mixture is a golden color, then add the rest of the crème and the mustard. Season with salt and a lot of pepper. Bring to a boil and cook, stirring, to thicken the sauce.
4. Add the meat strips and any juices from the frying pan and heat through quickly, stirring. Do not let the mixture boil again. Serve immediately.

Entrecôtes bordelaise

Rib Steaks in Bordelaise Sauce

🔪 00:15		00:05 to 00:10 🥘
American	**Ingredients**	**Metric/Imperial**
1 tbsp	Oil	1 tbsp
⅔ cup	Butter	150 g / 5 oz
6 (½ lb)	Boneless rib [sirloin or entrecôte] steaks	6 (250 g / 8 oz)
6	Shallots	6
½	Bottle red wine (preferably Bordeaux)	½
1	Fresh thyme sprig	1
1	Bay leaf	1
	Salt and pepper	
1	Small bunch of fresh parsley	1
½	Lemon	½

1. Heat the oil with ¼ cup [50 g / 2 oz] of the butter in a frying pan. Add the steaks and cook over a high heat for 2-4 minutes on each side, according to taste. When they are cooked, arrange them on a warmed serving platter and keep hot.

2. Discard the fat left in the frying pan. Peel and finely chop the shallots. Put them in the frying pan with the wine, thyme, bay leaf, and salt and pepper to taste. Bring to a boil, scraping the bottom of the pan to loosen the sediment. Reduce by at least half over a high heat.

3. Chop the parsley. Squeeze the juice from the ½ lemon. Strain the sauce and add the lemon juice, parsley and the remaining butter, cut into small pieces. Whisk the sauce well.

4. Pour the sauce over the hot steaks and serve immediately.

Chateaubriands béarnaise

Chateaubriand with Béarnaise Sauce

00:20　　　00:25

American	Ingredients	Metric/Imperial
2	Shallots	2
2	Fresh tarragon sprigs	2
2	Fresh chervil sprigs	2
¾ cup + 1 tbsp	Butter	190 g / 6½ oz
1 tbsp	Oil	1 tbsp
⅔ cup	Vinegar	150 ml / ¼ pint
	Salt and pepper	
3	Egg yolks, at room temperature	3
2 tbsp	Water	2 tbsp
6 (½ lb)	Chateaubriand steaks (from thickest part of beef tenderloin or fillet)	6 (250 g / 8 oz)

1. Peel and finely chop the shallots. Chop the tarragon and chervil leaves.

2. Heat 1 tablespoon [15 g / ½ oz] of butter with the oil in a heavy saucepan. Add the shallots, half of the tarragon and chervil, the vinegar and pepper to taste. Reduce over a gentle heat for 20 minutes (put a heatproof mat under the pan to diffuse the heat) until only 1 tablespoon of vinegar remains.

3. Meanwhile, heat the rest of the butter in a bowl placed over a pan of hot water or in a double boiler. When the butter has melted you will see a whitish deposit at the bottom: this is the whey. Pour the melted butter very carefully into a bowl so as to leave the whey behind.

4. Preheat the broiler [grill].

5. Put the egg yolks into another bowl over the pan of hot water. Add the reduced vinegar mixture, beating with a whisk. Gradually whisk in the water, a pinch of salt and some pepper and whisk until the mixture becomes creamy. Remove from the heat and, still whisking, dribble in the melted butter. Strain the sauce, then stir in the rest of the tarragon and chervil. Keep warm over the pan of hot water.

6. Cook the steaks under the broiler for 3-5 minutes on each side, depending on whether you like them rare, medium or well done.

7. Serve the steaks accompanied by the hot béarnaise sauce.

Boeuf miroton

Beef in Onion Sauce

00:20   00:50

American	Ingredients	Metric/Imperial
¾ lb	Onions	350 g / 12 oz
1½ lb	Cooked beef	750 g / 1½ lb
3 tbsp	Oil	3 tbsp
2 cups	Beef stock	450 ml / ¾ pint
⅔ cup	Vinegar	150 ml / ¼ pint
2 tbsp	Sliced dill pickles [gherkins]	2 tbsp
	Salt and pepper	

1. Peel and thinly slice the onions. Slice the cooked beef. Heat the oil in a flameproof casserole, add the onions and cook until they are translucent but not colored.
2. Add the beef stock and vinegar and bring to a boil. Boil for 15 minutes, stirring occasionally, until the mixture has taken on the consistency of cream.
3. Add the beef slices. Cover and cook gently, without letting it boil, for 10 minutes.
4. Add the gherkins, and salt and pepper to taste.

Entrecôtes bercy

Rib Steaks in Bercy Sauce

00:10   00:20

American	Ingredients	Metric/Imperial
6	Shallots	6
1 cup	Dry white wine	250 ml / 8 fl oz
	Salt and pepper	
6 (½ lb)	Boneless rib [sirloin or entrecôte] steaks	6 (250 g / 8 oz)
2 - 3 tbsp	Oil	2 - 3 tbsp
1	Bunch of fresh parsley	1
6 tbsp	Butter	75 g / 3 oz

1. Peel and finely chop the shallots. Put them in a small saucepan with the wine and salt and pepper. Cook over a medium heat until only 2-3 tablespoons of liquid remain.
2. Meanwhile, heat a steak or chop grill or griddle. Brush the steaks with the oil, lay them on the grill and cook for 3-4 minutes on each side. Season with salt and pepper.
3. Chop the parsley. When the shallot sauce has reduced, add the chopped parsley and the butter cut into small pieces, whisking well.
4. Serve the steaks coated with the sauce.

Cook's tip: add the salt to the steaks as each side is browned.

Pork

Jambon au champagne

Ham with Champagne Sauce

	00:30 plus soaking		03:00 Serves 10-12

American	Ingredients	Metric/Imperial
1 (6½ lb)	Piece uncooked country ham	1 (3 kg / 6½ lb)
2	Shallots	2
2	Onions	2
2	Garlic cloves	2
2	Carrots	2
1	Bouquet garni	1
1	Bottle of brut champagne	1
	Confectioners' [icing] sugar	
1 tbsp	Potato starch or flour or cornstarch [cornflour]	1 tbsp
1 tsp	Tomato paste [purée]	1 tsp
	Salt and pepper	

1. Soak the ham for 18-24 hours in cold water to cover, to remove excess salt, changing the water 2 or 3 times. Drain.

2. Peel the shallots, onions, garlic cloves and carrots. Place them in a large flameproof casserole, add the ham and bouquet garni, and cover with cold water. Cover, bring to a boil over a moderate heat and simmer for 1½ hours.

3. Preheat the oven to 425°F / 220°C / Gas Mark 7.

4. Drain the ham, discarding the cooking liquid and vegetables. Remove the rind and excess fat from the ham. Put the ham back in the casserole and pour over the champagne. Place in the oven and cook for 1-1½ hours, basting frequently. The ham will be cooked when the small shank [knuckle] bone can be pulled out but offers a slight resistance.

5. Remove the ham from the casserole. Place it in a roasting pan and sprinkle it with confectioners' [icing] sugar. Increase the oven temperature to 450°F / 230°C / Gas Mark 8, return the ham to the oven and cook until it is golden.

6. Meanwhile, boil to reduce the champagne in the casserole. Add the potato starch or cornstarch, dissolved in 1 tablespoon cold water, and the tomato paste and stir well. Taste the sauce and adjust the seasoning.

7. Serve the ham carved into slices, with a little sauce poured over. Serve the rest of the sauce in a sauceboat.

Chipolatas au vin blanc

Sausages with Rich Wine Sauce

| | 00:15 | | 00:25 | |

American	Ingredients	Metric/Imperial
1 tbsp	Butter	15 g / ½ oz
12	Thin pork sausages [chipolatas], 5 in / 12 cm long	12
2	Shallots	2
1 ½ cups	Dry white wine	350 ml / 12 fl oz
1 tbsp	Oil	1 tbsp
6	Slices of white bread	6
2	Egg yolks	2
1 tbsp	Crème fraîche	1 tbsp
	Salt and pepper	
1 tsp	Tomato paste [purée]	1 tsp
	Chopped fresh parsley for garnish	

1. Melt the butter in a small heavy-based frying pan, add the sausages, pricked with a fork so that they do not burst, and cook over a low heat for 10 minutes, turning to brown evenly. Remove and keep hot.

2. Peel and finely chop the shallots. Discard half the cooking fat from the frying pan, add the shallots and cook until translucent. Add the wine and boil to reduce by one-third over a moderate heat.

3. Meanwhile, heat the oil in another frying pan, add the slices of bread and fry until golden brown on both sides. Drain on paper towels.

4. Beat the egg yolks with the crème fraîche. Add to the sauce and allow to thicken over a low heat, stirring all the time. Do not boil. Season with salt and pepper. Stir in the tomato paste.

5. Arrange the sausages on the fried bread and sprinkle with chopped parsley. Serve with the sauce.

Lamb

Gigot grillé au beurre d'ail

Lamb Steaks with Garlic Butter

	00:10 plus chilling	00:08 to 00:12

American	Ingredients	Metric/Imperial
3	Garlic cloves	3
½ cup	Butter, at room temperature	125 g / 4 oz
	Salt and pepper	
6	Lamb leg steaks (slices cut from top of leg)	6
6 tbsp	Oil	6 tbsp

1. Peel the garlic and crush as finely as possible using a mortar and pestle or with the blade of a knife. Mix with the butter. Season with salt and pepper. Roll the garlic butter into a cylindrical shape. Wrap in foil and chill until firm.
2. Preheat the broiler [grill].
3. Brush the lamb steaks with the oil. Place the steaks on the rack of the broiler pan and cook for 4-6 minutes on each side, according to taste.
4. Cut the garlic butter into 6 or 12 slices and place 1 or 2 on each lamb steak. Serve hot.

Lamb-chop

Lamb Chops with Herb Butter

	00:05	00:05 to 00:10

American	Ingredients	Metric/Imperial
½ cup	Butter, at room temperature	125 g / 4 oz
2 tbsp	Chopped fresh herbs (chives, parsley, tarragon)	2 tbsp
1	Garlic clove	1
6 (5 oz)	Thin lamb loin double chops	6 (150 g / 5 oz)
	Salt and pepper	

1. Mash all but 2 tablespoons (25 g / 1 oz) of the butter with the herbs and peeled and crushed garlic. Chill until firm.
2. Melt the remaining butter in a large frying pan. Add the chops to the pan — in one layer — and cook for 5-10 minutes according to taste, turning over halfway through. Keep a close eye on how the 'tails' of the chops are cooking; they should not be cooked as much as the thicker meat.
3. Arrange the chops on a warmed serving dish. Sprinkle with salt and pepper and top each chop with a spoonful of the seasoned butter. Serve hot.

Blanquette d'agneau

Lamb in a White Sauce

	00:15		00:45

American	Ingredients	Metric/Imperial
2 lb	Boneless breast of lamb	1 kg / 2 lb
1	Onion	1
2 tbsp	Oil	2 tbsp
1	Carrot	1
1	Bouquet garni	1
1¼ cups	Water	300 ml / ½ pint
	Salt and pepper	
1 tbsp	Butter	15 g / ½ oz
1 tbsp	Flour	1 tbsp
1	Egg yolk	1
2 tbsp	Crème fraîche	2 tbsp

1. Cut the lamb into cubes. Peel and thinly slice the onion. Heat the oil in a flameproof casserole, add the onion and cook until golden. Add the lamb cubes and cook over a moderate heat for a few minutes, without letting them color.
2. Meanwhile, peel and slice the carrot. Add this to the casserole with the bouquet garni and water. Season with salt and pepper and stir well. Cook over a medium heat for 40 minutes.
3. Remove the meat with a slotted spoon and keep warm on a serving dish. Strain the cooking liquid and set aside.
4. Melt the butter in a small saucepan over a low heat, add the flour and stir well until the butter has absorbed the flour. Gradually add the strained cooking liquid, stirring well. Cook over a gentle heat for 5 minutes until thick, stirring constantly. Remove from the heat.
5. Mix the egg yolk in a bowl with the crème fraîche. Season with salt and pepper. Add this mixture to the sauce, stirring briskly.
6. Pour the sauce over the meat and serve hot.

Veal

Estouffade à la moutarde

Veal in Wine and Mustard Sauce

	00:20	02:15	

American	Ingredients	Metric/Imperial
2 lb	Boneless breast of veal	1 kg / 2 lb
1 lb	Boned veal blade steaks [middle neck cutlets]	500 g / 1 lb
¼ lb	Lightly salted lean bacon	125 g / 4 oz
¼ lb	Bacon rind	125 g / 4 oz
4	Shallots	4
½ lb	Button mushrooms	250 g / 8 oz
½	Lemon	½
3 tbsp	Oil	3 tbsp
2 tbsp	Butter	25 g / 1 oz
1 tbsp	Flour	1 tbsp
1 cup	Dry white wine	250 ml / 8 fl oz
1 tbsp	Prepared mustard	1 tbsp
1	Fresh thyme sprig	1
1	Bay leaf	1
1 cup	Thin crème fraîche	250 ml / 8 fl oz
	Salt and pepper	

1. Preheat the oven to 350°F / 180°C / Gas Mark 4.

2. Cut all the veal into large cubes. Cut the bacon and bacon rind into matchstick strips. Peel and finely chop the shallots. Thinly slice the mushrooms. Sprinkle them with the juice of the ½ lemon and put to one side.

3. Heat the oil in a frying pan, add the veal and bacon and cook over a high heat for 5 minutes or until browned on all sides. Remove with a slotted spoon and place in a flameproof casserole.

4. Add the butter and shallots to the pan and cook over a medium heat for 3 minutes. Add to the casserole.

5. Sprinkle the flour over the casserole and mix in well. Add the wine, mustard, thyme, bay leaf, crème fraîche, mushrooms and their lemon juice, the bacon rind, and salt and pepper to taste. The meat should be completely covered; if it is not, add a little water. Mix everything together well.

6. Bring to a boil on top of the stove, then transfer the casserole to the oven. Cook for 2 hours or until the veal is tender.

Fricadelles au beurre

Rich Veal Patties

00:20   00:10

American	Ingredients	Metric/Imperial
2 cups	Bread crumbs	125 g / 4 oz
¼ cup	Crème fraîche	4 tbsp
1	Large onion	1
½ cup	Butter, at room temperature	125 g / 4 oz
2	Eggs	2
1 lb	Ground [minced] veal	500 g / 1 lb
	Salt and pepper	
	Grated nutmeg	
3 tbsp	Oil	3 tbsp

1. Put the bread crumbs in a small saucepan and add the crème fraîche. Heat gently, stirring, to make a sticky paste. Remove from the heat.
2. Peel and finely chop the onion. Melt 2 tablespoons [25 g / 1 oz] of the butter in a frying pan, add the onion and cook over a gentle heat, stirring, until it becomes translucent.
3. Break the eggs into a large mixing bowl. Add the veal, the rest of the butter, the bread crumb paste and the onion. Season with salt, pepper and a pinch of nutmeg. Mix well with the hands, then shape into 6 patties.
4. Heat the oil in a frying pan, add the patties and cook for 3 minutes on each side over a medium heat or until browned and cooked through. Serve hot.

Escalopes au cidre

Scaloppine with Cider Cream

00:10   00:20

American	Ingredients	Metric/Imperial
3	Onions	3
6 (5 oz)	Veal scaloppine [escalopes]	6 (150 g / 5 oz)
	Salt and pepper	
3 tbsp	Butter	40 g / 1 ½ oz
2 ½ cups	Dry hard cider	600 ml / 1 pint
1 ½ cups	Crème fraîche	350 ml / 12 fl oz

1. Peel and finely chop the onions. Sprinkle the slices of veal with salt and pepper on both sides. Melt the butter in a frying pan, add the veal and cook for 4-5 minutes on each side, until golden brown. Remove and keep hot.
2. Add the onions to the pan and cook for about 5 minutes over a medium heat, scraping up the meat residue from the bottom of the pan with a wooden spatula. Pour in the cider and reduce over a high heat until only about 3 tablespoons of liquid remain.
3. Reduce the heat and add the crème fraîche. Reduce by half, stirring constantly. Season with salt and pepper.
4. Return the veal to the pan and reheat briefly in the sauce.

VEGETABLES

Brocolis au gratin

Broccoli in Cheese Sauce

American	Ingredients	Metric/Imperial
	Salt and pepper	
2 lb	Broccoli	1 kg / 2 lb
¼ cup	Butter	50 g / 2 oz
2 tbsp	Flour	25 g / 1 oz
2 cups	Milk	500 ml / ¾ pint
⅔ cup	Crème fraîche	150 ml / ¼ pint
	Grated nutmeg	
1 cup	Grated gruyère cheese	125 g / 4 oz

1. Boil some salted water in a saucepan.

2. Thoroughly wash the broccoli and trim. Add to the pan and cook for about 10 minutes or until just tender.

3. Drain well and chop into large pieces. Preheat the oven to 400°F / 200°C / Gas Mark 6.

4. Melt 2 tablespoons [25 g / 1 oz] of the butter in a frying pan. Add the broccoli and cook gently to evaporate any remaining water. Season with salt and pepper. Remove the pan from the heat.

5. Melt the remaining butter in a heavy-bottomed saucepan over a low heat. Add the flour and mix together until the butter has absorbed all the flour. Gradually add the milk and continue stirring over a low heat for about 10 minutes or until the sauce thickens. Finally, stir in the crème fraîche, a pinch of nutmeg and half the gruyère and season with salt and pepper.

6. Arrange the broccoli in a gratin dish, pour over the cheese sauce and sprinkle with the remaining cheese. Bake for 20-30 minutes or until golden brown. Serve hot.

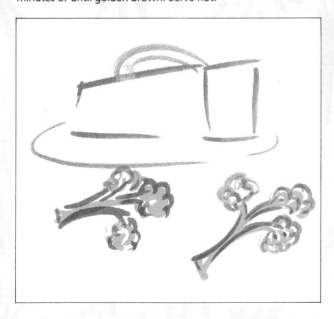

Concombres au gratin

Cucumbers in Cheese Sauce

	00:30		00:30	

American	Ingredients	Metric/Imperial
3	Cucumbers	3
	Salt and pepper	
1	Onion	1
2 tbsp	Butter	25 g / 1 oz
2 tbsp	Flour	25 g / 1 oz
¾ cup	Crème fraîche	200 ml / 7 fl oz
½ cup	Grated gruyère cheese	50 g / 2 oz
	Grated nutmeg	

1. Preheat the oven to 425°F / 220°C / Gas Mark 7.
2. Peel the cucumbers and cut into quarters, lengthwise. Remove the seeds and dice the flesh.
3. Add the cubes of cucumber to a pan of boiling salted water and blanch for 10-12 minutes. Drain and place in a gratin dish.
4. Peel and finely chop the onion. Heat the butter in a saucepan, add the onion and cook over a low heat, without browning. Sprinkle in the flour, mix well and add the crème fraîche, stirring constantly until the mixture has thickened. Stir in the grated cheese, a small pinch of nutmeg and salt and pepper to taste.
5. Pour the sauce over the cucumber. Bake for 20 minutes until the top is golden brown.

Cook's tip: this first course also goes well with roasts.

Épinards béchamel

Spinach with Béchamel Sauce

	00:15		00:30	

American	Ingredients	Metric/Imperial
5 lb	Fresh spinach	2.5 kg / 5 lb
	Salt and pepper	
3 cups	Béchamel sauce	750 ml / 1 ¼ pints
	Grated nutmeg	

1. Preheat the oven to 425°F / 220°C / Gas Mark 7.
2. Remove the stems from the spinach and wash the leaves thoroughly. Put in a large saucepan with a large pinch of salt (no extra water should be needed) and cook over a medium heat for 8 minutes, stirring occasionally. Drain well.
3. Butter an ovenproof dish. Put half the spinach in the bottom of the dish and cover with half the sauce. Add another layer of spinach and top with the remaining sauce.
4. Bake for 10 minutes until golden brown. Serve very hot.

Cook's tip: add a soft-boiled or poached egg to each serving for a quick lunch or supper dish; or sprinkle with grated gruyère cheese for extra goodness.

Purée de chicorée

Chicory [Curly Endive] Purée

| | 00:20 | | 00:25 | |

American	Ingredients	Metric/Imperial
4 lb	Chicory [curly endive]	2 kg / 4 lb
	Salt and pepper	
2 tbsp	Butter	60 g / 2 oz
1½ cups	Béchamel sauce	350 ml / 12 fl oz
4	Slices of bread ½ in / 1 cm thick	4

1. Remove any damaged leaves from the chicory, cut into quarters and wash. Boil some salted water in a saucepan, add the chicory and simmer for 15 minutes.
2. Drain the chicory well and put it through a blender, vegetable mill or food processor. Add to the béchamel sauce. Taste and adjust the seasoning if necessary. Pour into a warmed serving dish and keep hot.
3. Melt the butter in a frying pan and fry the slices of bread until golden brown on both sides. Cut into small cubes and arrange on the chicory. Serve immediately.

Cook's tip: although this vegetable is more usually served raw in salads, it is equally good cooked. Try this delicious alternative as an accompaniment to crisp bacon.

Pain de laitue

Lettuce Loaf

| | 00:45 | | 00:45 | |

American	Ingredients	Metric/Imperial
	Salt and pepper	
3	Heads of soft-leaved lettuce	3
4	Eggs	4
2½ cups	Béchamel sauce	600 ml / 1 pint
	Grated nutmeg	
2	Slices of cooked ham	2

1. Preheat the oven to 350°F / 180°C / Gas Mark 4.
2. Bring a saucepan of salted water to a boil. Cut the heads of lettuce in half and plunge into the boiling water. Cook for 2 minutes. Drain well. Chop the lettuce finely.
3. Break the eggs into a bowl and beat well. Add the lettuce and half the sauce. Mix well.
4. Butter an 8 in / 20 cm savarin mold. Cut the slices of ham into triangles and arrange in the bottom of the mold. Pour the lettuce mixture into the mold and place in a large ovenproof dish. Fill the dish with water to halfway up the sides of the mold.
5. Bake for 45 minutes.
6. To serve, turn out of the mold and cover with the remaining béchamel sauce.

Gratin de courgettes au riz

Zucchini [Courgettes] and Rice

▭▭▷ 00:25		00:40 ⌔
American	**Ingredients**	**Metric/Imperial**
4 lb	Zucchini [courgettes]	2 kg / 4 lb
	Salt and pepper	
3 tbsp	Long-grain rice	3 tbsp
3	Eggs	3
1 cup	Crème fraîche	250 ml / 8 fl oz
1¾ cups	Grated cheese	200 g / 7 oz
	Grated nutmeg	

1. Preheat the oven to 350°F / 180°C / Gas Mark 4.

2. Cut the zucchini into thick slices. Cook for about 5 minutes in a little salted water and drain well.

3. Arrange in a gratin dish and sprinkle with the rice.

4. In a bowl beat the eggs with the crème fraîche and the grated cheese. Flavor with a pinch of nutmeg and season with salt and pepper.

5. Pour the sauce over the zucchini and mix well together.

6. Bake for 40 minutes or until the rice has absorbed the water from the zucchini and the top is lightly browned.

Galettes de pomme de terre

Creamed Potato Cakes

▭▭▷ 00:20		00:35 ⌔
American	**Ingredients**	**Metric/Imperial**
1½ lb	Potatoes	750 g / 1½ lb
	Salt and pepper	
1 cup	Milk	250 ml / 8 fl oz
3 tbsp	Flour	3 tbsp
6	Eggs	6
5 tbsp	Crème fraîche	5 tbsp
⅔ cup	Butter	150 g / 5 oz

1. Peel and cut up the potatoes. Place in a saucepan, cover with cold salted water and cook over a brisk heat for 30 minutes. Drain.

2. Heat the milk in a saucepan. Mash the potatoes and add the hot milk. Season with salt and pepper to taste. Mix thoroughly with a wooden spatula and leave to cool.

3. When the potato is cold add the flour and mix well. Then work in the eggs one at a time together with the crème fraîche. Mix thoroughly. Take one tablespoon of the potato mixture at a time and shape into a flat cake.

4. Melt the butter in a frying pan. When the butter is very hot fry the potato cakes for 1 minute each side and serve immediately.

Pommes surprises

Spinach Soufflé Potatoes

	00:15	01:50

American	Ingredients	Metric/Imperial
6	Very large potatoes	6
1 lb	Spinach, fresh or frozen	500 g / 1 lb
½ cup	Butter	125 g / 4 oz
	Salt and pepper	
½ cup	Crème fraîche	125 ml / 4 fl oz
	Grated nutmeg	
8	Eggs	8

1. Preheat the oven to 350°F / 180°C / Gas Mark 4.
2. Scrub the potatoes, prick all over and wrap each separately in foil. Bake for 1½ hours.
3. Meanwhile, wash the spinach thoroughly — if using fresh — and remove the stems. Put the leaves in a large pan and cook for about 8 minutes. If using frozen spinach allow 10 minutes extra cooking time to allow the spinach to thaw. Drain well.
4. Chop the spinach, return to the pan and place over a low heat. Add three-quarters of the butter and season with salt and pepper. Cook to evaporate any excess liquid, then remove from the heat.
5. When the potatoes are cooked, open the foil, cut the top off each potato and remove most of the flesh with a teaspoon, taking care not to break the skins. Put the flesh to one side.
6. Fill the bottom of each potato shell with 2 tablespoons of spinach. Add 1 tablespoon of crème fraîche and a little freshly grated nutmeg to each potato. Season with salt and pepper. Break an egg into each potato and sprinkle with a little salt.
7. Separate the remaining eggs. Mash the potato flesh and mix in the remaining butter and the egg yolks. Beat the egg whites until stiff and fold into the mixture. Season with salt and pepper.
8. Cover each potato with this mixture and arrange in a buttered baking dish. Return to the oven and bake for 20 minutes until the tops are golden brown.

Topinambours sauce béchamel

Jerusalem Artichokes with Béchamel

	00:15	00:40

American	Ingredients	Metric/Imperial
2 lb	Jerusalem artichokes	1 kg / 2 lb
	Salt and pepper	
2 cups	Béchamel sauce	500 ml / ¾ pint
	Grated nutmeg	

1. Peel the artichokes and cook in a small amount of boiling, salted water for 15-20 minutes.
2. Drain the artichokes and add to the sauce. Simmer gently for 10 minutes and serve very hot.

Gratin dauphinois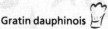

Dauphinois Potatoes

	00:25	01:00 to 01:30

American	Ingredients	Metric/Imperial
2 lb	Waxy potatoes	1 kg / 2 lb
1¼ cups	Milk	300 ml / ½ pint
1	Garlic clove	1
	Butter	
2	Eggs	2
⅔ cup	Crème fraîche	150 ml / ¼ pint
	Salt and pepper	
	Grated nutmeg	
1¼ cups	Grated gruyère cheese	150 g / 5 oz

1. Preheat the oven to 350°F / 180°C / Gas Mark 4.
2. Peel the potatoes and wipe dry, then cut into thin slices. Heat the milk.
3. Peel the garlic and rub around the inside of a shallow ovenproof dish. Generously butter the dish.
4. Beat together the eggs, crème fraîche and warm milk. Season with salt and pepper and a little freshly grated nutmeg.
5. Cover the bottom of the dish with a layer of potato, sprinkle with a little grated cheese and moisten with a little of the crème mixture. Repeat until you have used all the ingredients, ending with a layer of cheese.
6. Bake for 1-1½ hours until the potatoes are tender and the top is golden brown.

Cook's tip: an authentic Dauphinois Potatoes contains no gruyère cheese, but this does add extra flavor.

Oseille à la crème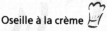

Sorrel with Cream

	00:15	00:30

American	Ingredients	Metric/Imperial
2 lb	Sorrel	1 kg / 2 lb
	Salt and pepper	
⅓ cup	Butter	75 g / 3 oz
⅔ cup	Crème fraîche	150 ml / ¼ pint

1. Remove the stems from the sorrel and wash the leaves. Bring a saucepan of salted water to a boil. Add the sorrel and cook for 5 minutes. Drain well.
2. Melt the butter in a frying pan, add the sorrel and cook for 10-15 minutes, stirring constantly. Season with salt and pepper and add the crème fraîche. Stir over a moderate heat until the sauce thickens. Adjust the seasoning if necessary and serve immediately.

DESSERTS

Crème anglaise
Vanilla Custard Sauce

00:05
plus cooling   Makes about 1 quart 1 l / 1¾ pints
00:15

American	Ingredients	Metric/Imperial
1 quart	Milk	1 l / 1¾ pints
1	Vanilla bean [pod] or	1
	Vanilla extract [essence]	
	Salt	
8 - 10	Egg yolks	8 - 10
¾ cup	Superfine [caster] sugar	150 g / 5 oz

1. Place the milk in a saucepan and add the vanilla bean, cut in half lengthwise, or a few drops of vanilla extract, and a pinch of salt. Bring to a boil, then remove from the heat and leave to infuse.

2. Beat together the egg yolks and sugar until the mixture becomes pale. Remove the vanilla bean from the milk and gradually whisk the milk into the eggs. Pour the mixture back into the pan and cook over a low heat for about 10 minutes, stirring constantly. On no account allow the custard to boil.

3. As soon as the custard is thick enough to coat a spoon, remove the pan from the heat and leave to cool, stirring from time to time to prevent a skin forming.

Cook's tip: if you are afraid of the custard separating, beat 1 teaspoon of flour or cornstarch [cornflour] with the egg yolks. This custard is the basis of many desserts and ice creams.

Crème Chantilly
Chantilly Cream

00:20
plus chilling
00:00

American	Ingredients	Metric/Imperial
2 cups	Thin crème fraîche	500 ml / ¾ pint
½ cup	Confectioners' [icing] sugar	50 g / 2 oz
	Vanilla extract [essence]	

1. The whole secret of this recipe's success lies in the correct temperature of the cream: place the crème fraîche in the bowl in which you intend to whip it, in the refrigerator 2 hours in advance.

2. Whip the cream gently until it doubles in volume and sticks to the blades of the beater. Do not whip too quickly or you risk turning the cream into butter.

3. With a wooden spoon slowly stir in the sugar, then a few drops of vanilla and mix well.

4. Chill until ready to serve.

Cook's tip: if you prefer to use thick crème fraîche, add some very cold milk (allowing 5 tablespoons milk to 1 cup [250 ml / 8 fl oz] crème fraîche).

Crème renversée au chocolat

Upside-down Chocolate Custard

	00:30 plus chilling		01:15
American	**Ingredients**	**Metric/Imperial**	
8 oz	Semisweet [plain] chocolate	250 g / 8 oz	
2 tbsp	Water	2 tbsp	
1 quart	Milk	1 l / 1 ¾ pints	
	Vanilla extract [essence]		
5	Eggs	5	
5	Egg yolks	5	
2 tbsp	Sugar	2 tbsp	
1 quantity	Vanilla custard sauce	1 quantity	

1. Preheat the oven to 325°F / 160°C / Gas Mark 3.
2. Break the chocolate into a bowl and add the water. Place over a pan of hot water to melt.
3. Meanwhile, bring the milk and a few drops of vanilla extract to a boil. In a mixing bowl, beat the whole eggs and egg yolks, then vigorously beat in the hot milk. Stir in the melted chocolate and add the sugar (this custard should not be too sweet).
4. Strain the custard into a 1 quart [1 l / 1¾ pint] charlotte mold. Place the mold in a shallow ovenproof dish and fill the dish to halfway up the mold with water.
5. Bake for 1 hour or until a skewer inserted into the center of the custard comes out clean.
6. Remove the mold from the dish in the oven and leave to cool. Chill for at least 6 hours.
7. When ready to serve, loosen the custard and unmold it onto a serving dish. Top with the cold vanilla custard sauce.

Crème au kirsch

Kirsch Custard

	00:20 plus cooling		00:10
American	**Ingredients**	**Metric/Imperial**	
1 quart	Milk	1 l / 1 ¾ pints	
1	Vanilla bean [pod]	1	
	Salt		
6	Egg yolks	6	
1 cup	Flour	125 g / 4 oz	
1 cup	Sugar	250 g / 8 oz	
½ quantity	Chantilly cream	½ quantity	
¼ cup	Kirsch	4 tbsp	

1. Bring the milk to a boil with the halved vanilla bean and a pinch of salt. Remove from the heat and leave to infuse.
2. Meanwhile, beat the egg yolks with the flour and sugar. Remove the vanilla bean from the milk, and beat the milk into the egg yolk mixture. Return to the milk pan.
3. Return to a gentle heat and bring to a boil, stirring until the custard thickens.

4. Strain the custard into a bowl. Grease a piece of foil with butter and place on the surface of the custard to prevent a skin forming.

5. Just before serving fold in the chantilly cream and kirsch.

Soufflé à l'orange

Orange Liqueur Soufflé

| | 00:25 | | 00:40 | |

American	Ingredients	Metric/Imperial
2	Oranges	2
½ quantity	Vanilla custard sauce	½ quantity
1 ¼ cups	Mandarin or orange liqueur	300 ml / ½ pint
½ quantity	Pastry cream	½ quantity
4	Egg whites	4
12	Ladyfingers [sponge fingers]	12

1. Preheat the oven to 425°F / 220°C / Gas Mark 7.

2. Thinly pare the rind from 1 orange. Add to the custard sauce with 4 tablespoons of the liqueur. Set aside in the refrigerator.

3. Finely grate the rind from the remaining orange and squeeze out the juice. Stir the grated rind and juice into the pastry cream.

4. Beat the egg whites until stiff and fold carefully into the pastry cream.

5. Moisten the lady fingers with the remaining liqueur.

6. Butter a 6 in / 15 cm soufflé dish. Cover the bottom with a layer of ladyfingers, then add a layer of pastry cream. Continue the layers until you have used all the ingredients, finishing with a layer of the cream.

7. Bake for 25-30 minutes.

8. Remove the orange rind from the custard sauce and serve with the soufflé immediately it is removed from the oven.

Oranges meringuées

Meringue Oranges

	00:50	00:20 to 00:25
	plus chilling	

American	Ingredients	Metric/Imperial
6	Oranges	6
1 cup	Raspberries (or pitted [stoned] cherries)	100 g / 4 oz
2	Bananas	2
2	Apples	2
1	Pear	1
½ cup	Granulated sugar	100 g / 4 oz
3	Egg whites	3
⅔ cup	Superfine [caster] sugar	150 g / 5 oz
1 cup	Crème fraîche or chantilly cream	250 ml / 8 fl oz

1. Cut a lid off each orange and remove the flesh without breaking the skins. Dice the flesh. Place the skins in an ovenproof dish and set aside.

2. Rinse, drain and hull the raspberries (or cherries). Peel and slice the bananas. Peel, core and slice the apples and pear. Place all the fruit in a bowl and sprinkle with the granulated sugar. Leave to steep in the refrigerator for 2 hours.

3. Preheat the oven to 275°F / 120°C / Gas Mark 1.

4. Pile the fruit salad into the orange skins.

5. Beat the egg whites, gradually adding the superfine sugar, until stiff. Transfer the meringue to a pastry bag and pipe onto the tops of the oranges. Take care that the fruit is completely covered.

6. Bake for about 25 minutes, without allowing the meringue to brown. Serve at once with crème fraîche or chantilly cream.

Mont blanc

Chestnut Cream Cake

	01:30	00:30

American	Ingredients	Metric/Imperial
¾ cup + 2 tbsp	Butter	200 g / 7 oz
3	Eggs, separated	3
1	Egg yolk	1
6 tbsp	Superfine [caster] sugar	75 g / 3 oz
¾ cup	Flour	75 g / 3 oz
¼ cup	Rum	4 tbsp
1½ lb	Canned sweetened chestnut purée	750 g / 1½ lb
1 tbsp	Cocoa powder	1 tbsp
½ cup	Granulated sugar	125 g / 4 oz
⅓ cup	Water	5 tbsp
1 quantity	Chantilly cream	1 quantity

1. Preheat the oven to 450°F / 230°C / Gas Mark 8.

2. Melt 2 tablespoons [25 g / 1 oz] butter. Set aside. Beat the 4 egg yolks with half the superfine sugar. When pale, quickly work in the flour. Beat the 3 egg whites until very stiff and gradually beat in the remaining superfine sugar. Beat the egg whites and melted butter into the egg yolk mixture.

3. Pour the batter into a buttered 10 in / 25 cm cake pan. Bake for about 10 minutes or until a skewer inserted into the center of the cake comes out clean. Remove the cake from the oven, unmold and leave to cool.

4. Mix half the rum with the chestnut purée in a warm bowl. Add the remaining butter and the cocoa. Beat well until smooth.

5. Put the chestnut paste into a pastry bag fitted with a plain ¼ in / 5 mm nozzle. Pipe over the sides of an oiled 10 in / 25 cm savarin mold in successive rings. Leave in the refrigerator to set.

6. Cut the cake into 2 layers.

7. Dissolve the granulated sugar in the water and remaining rum. Bring to a boil and boil for 2 minutes. Moisten the two cake layers with this syrup, and break one layer into pieces.

8. Place the whole cake layer on a flat serving plate. Slide the chestnut case out of the savarin mold and place the case on the cake layer. Fill the chestnut case with alternate layers of broken cake and chantilly cream. Place the rest of the chantilly cream in a pastry bag fitted with a plain ½ in / 1 cm nozzle and pipe the cream over the whole cake. Serve at once.

Glace au citron

Lemon Ice Cream

	00:10 *plus freezing*		00:00

American	Ingredients	Metric/Imperial
5	Lemons	5
1 quart	Water	1 l / 1¾ pints
1½ cups	Sugar	350 g / 12 oz
¼ cup	Thick crème fraîche	4 tbsp

1. Finely grate the rind of 1 lemon into a bowl. Squeeze the juice of the 5 lemons and strain into the bowl. Add the water, sugar and crème fraîche. Mix thoroughly.

2. Pour the mixture into an ice cream maker and freeze according to the manufacturer's instructions.

3. Transfer the ice cream to the refrigerator about 20 minutes before serving.

4. Serve the ice cream on its own with raspberry sauce or a syrup.

INDEX